Readers' Praise for John Gatto's *A Different Kind of Teacher*

"Gatto is an inspiring author and teacher. . . . He probes for solutions to difficult educational problems with an eye to how things are, how they could be, and what needs to be done to reach new goals. This volume is an eye opening to those inside and out of education. Recommended at all levels."
— CHOICE

"Provocative, stimulating, evocative, and consistent: such is this collection of comments clarifying the ills of American public education and ideas for solving them. . . . Written in an informative, easy-to-understand, and prophetic style, this work nicely complements Gatto's other titles."
— *Library Journal*

"I happen to agree with damn near every semi-colon and comma that Mr. Gatto has written."
— Tom Peters, author of *In Seach of Excellence* and *The Brand You 50*

"Exceptional !!!!" (2001 "Best Read" selection)
— *Today's Books*

"John Gatto's writing is like a Jackson Pollock painting — a streak of history here, a splash of humor there, three drops of statistics. Every sentence is filled with passion. You have to work hard to understand what John Gatto is getting at, but the reward is an invitation to an endless adventure; the search for meaning in life."
— *Education Revolution*

D1557166

A DIFFERENT KIND OF TEACHER

Solving the Crisis of American Schooling

JOHN TAYLOR GATTO

Berkeley Hills Books
Berkeley, California

Published by
Berkeley Hills Books
P. O. Box 9877
Berkeley, California 94709
www.berkeleyhills.com
(888) 848-7303

Comments on this book may also be addressed to: jpstroh@berkeleyhills.com

Cover design by Elysium, San Francisco.
Cover photo by Anonymous. Rights reserved.
Manufactured in the United States of America.
Distributed by Publishers Group West.

Library of Congress Cataloging-in-Publication Data

(Available from the Publisher)

Contents

Introduction

On July 25, 1991 *The Wall Street Journal* published an op-ed contribution from a veteran Manhattan public school teacher, John Taylor Gatto. The short, passionate essay, "I May Be a Teacher But I'm Not an Educator," written by a man recently named New York State Teacher of the Year and, for the third consecutive time, New York City Teacher of the Year, grabbed the attention of disillusioned parents, students, and teachers across the country, while serving as a shot across the bow for educational functionaries locked in the inertia of mediocrity.

Shortly after publication of this essay, Gatto resigned from his position as a seventh grade teacher at Booker T. Washington School on W. 107th Street, and in the decade since has been among the country's most penetrating, wise, irritating, informed, provocative, and prophetic voices in the fierce debate over education reform. His earlier book, *Dumbing Us Down: The Hidden Curriculum of Compulsory Schooling,* his dozens of published essays, and the hundreds of talks he has given — from The White House to homeschool coffee hours; from Bath, Maine to Beijing — have had a profound influence on the reinvention of our schools, and on the lives of hundreds of thousands, if not millions, of school children.

A Different Kind of Teacher brings together sixteen key essays and speeches produced by Gatto between 1990 and 1999. *Part One: Schoolrooms Speak Bluntly* includes three pieces written while he was still an active classroom teacher, and a short article written by one of his students, offering a glimpse at how Gatto translated his theories of education into the school setting. These writings, and the contexts in which they were presented, show the essence of Gatto's ideas on teaching practice, the real-world situations in which they were forged, and some of the institutional opposition one inevitably faces in implementing them.

Part Two: Analyzing the System includes seven papers written in the period after Gatto's resignation from public school teaching. They represent a critique of American schooling, filled with insights gleaned from three decades in the classroom combined with years of research into the history and philosophy of Western education. Although most readers will find his discoveries disturbing, the information Gatto has compiled here is arguably indispensable for understanding and repairing the pedagogical traditions we have inherited.

One essay in this section: *Horatio Alger's Country: The Mysterious Origins of American Adoption,* may at first glance appear to stray from the central subject of this collection. The relevance of this historical rumination, however, will be apparent to those who read it with the same openness and curiosity that Gatto brought to writing it.

Part Three: The Search for Meaning describes some of the results of Gatto's search for the purposes and goals of education and life. Although this section comes last in the book, the effort it records comes first in any serious exploration of what and how we teach our children. The conclusions Gatto arrives at will ring profoundly true with many. To others, they might at least show the way to find one's own contrary answers.

Although *A Different Kind of Teacher* is divided into three parts, each piece is driven by a similar search for solutions to difficult problems. Ideas and examples recur in new contexts that illuminate fresh perspectives. This book will have served its purpose if it functions like the best conversations, as Gatto describes them — if it helps readers to see more clearly what the American system of education really is, what it ought to be, and what steps can be taken to reach that goal.

The publishers would like to thank Tom Whelan for first bringing John Gatto's work into our sights; Jerry Brown, whose broadcast conversation with Mr. Gatto a few years ago convinced us of the power of his ideas; and Barbara Whiteside, without whose encouragement this book would never have happened.

For Briseis and Raven, who are never
out of my thoughts and prayers,
and never were and never will be.
Micans in tenebris agens.

Part One
Schoolrooms Speak Bluntly

The Curriculum of the Family

This essay originally appeared in Teacher *magazine in August 1990, as John Gatto's ideas and classroom successes were beginning to attract national attention. Gatto was at that time teaching seventh grade at Booker T. Washington School in New York City.*

I've noticed a fascinating phenomenon in my years of teaching: schools and schooling are increasingly irrelevant to the great enterprises of the planet. No one believes anymore that scientists are trained in science classes or politicians in civics classes or poets in English classes. The truth is that schools don't really teach anything except how to obey orders.

This is a great mystery to me because thousands of humane, caring people work in schools as teachers, aides, and administrators. It must be that the abstract logic of the institution overwhelms their individual contributions. Teachers do care and do work very hard, but the institution they work for is psychopathic; it has no conscience. It rings a bell and the young man in the middle of writing a poem must close his notebook and move to a different cell where he must memorize that man and monkeys evolved from a common ancestor.

Schools were designed by Horace Mann, E. L. Thorndike, and others to be instruments of the scientific management of a mass population. Schools are intended to produce, through the application of formulas, formulaic human beings whose behavior can be predicted and controlled. To a very great extent, schools succeed in doing this. But in a society that is increasingly fragmented, in which the only genuinely successful people are independent, self-reliant, confident, and individualistic, the products of school and "schooling" are irrelevant.

If we're going to change what is rapidly becoming a disaster of ignorance, we need to realize that the school as an institution "schools" very well, but it does not educate. As author Paul Goodman put it thirty years ago, we force children to grow up absurd, and any reform in schooling has to deal with its absurdities.

It is absurd and anti-life to be compelled to sit in confinement with people of exactly the same age and social class. This effectively cuts children off from the immense diversity of life and the synergy of variety. It cuts children off from their own past and future, sealing them in a continuous present much the same way television does.

It is absurd and anti-life to be forced to listen to a stranger reading poetry when you want to learn to construct buildings, or to be forced to sit with a stranger discussing the construction of buildings when you want to read poetry. It is absurd and anti-life to move from cell to cell at the sound of a gong every day of your natural youth in an institution that allows you no privacy and even follows you into the sanctuary of your home by demanding that you do its "homework."

Two institutions currently control our children's lives: television and schooling, in that order. Both of these reduce the real world of wisdom, fortitude, temperance, and justice to never-ending, nonstop abstractions.

In centuries past, children and adolescents would spend their time in real work, real charity, real adventures, and in the search for mentors who might teach them what they really wanted to learn. A great deal of time was spent in community pursuits, practicing affection, meeting and studying every level of the community, learning how to make a home, and performing dozens of other tasks necessary to becoming whole men and women.

But the children I teach have no time for these pursuits. After television, schooling, sleeping, and eating, they have only about nine hours each week to spend on growing up.

Is it any wonder that the children I teach are indifferent to the adult world, have almost no curiosity, and have a poor sense of the future, of how tomorrow is inextricably linked to today? Is it any wonder that the children I teach are often cruel to each other, lack compassion for misfortune, laugh at weakness, and have contempt for people whose need for help shows too plainly? Is it any wonder that the children I teach are uneasy with intimacy or candor and are materialistic, dependent, and passive in the face of new challenges?

This bleak picture can be altered only by changing the purpose of schooling. For schools to be worthwhile, they need worthwhile goals. Schools must:

• Create independent, resourceful, and fearless citizens,
• Tap the educational power of family life,
• Bestow significance on personal choices,
• Arrest the epidemic of alienation and loneliness,
• Restore democracy as a national mission,
• Reverse the growing isolation of social classes, and
• Regenerate communal life.

Schools can pursue these goals and still teach reading, writing, and arithmetic. Students can learn to think, speak, calculate, and write more easily through close contact with reality than through confinement and abstract texts.

We need to create a system of education that has as its core the belief that self-knowledge is the only basis for true knowledge. In such a system, a child will often be alone in an unguided setting with a problem to solve. Sometimes the problem is fraught with great risk, such as making a horse jump over a hurdle. Sometimes the problem poses more subtle challenges, such as mastering solitude, as Thoreau did.

Can you imagine children who master such challenges ever lacking confidence in themselves?

Consider the experience of one of my former students, Roland Legiardi-Laura. Although both his parents had died and left him with no inheritance, he rode a bicycle alone across the United States when he was hardly more than a boy. Is it any wonder that in manhood when Roland decided to make a film about Nicaragua — though he had no money and no prior experience in filmmaking — he made an international award-winner?

We need to breed that kind of commitment, sense of adventure, and independence in our children. To begin, we need to get students out of the classroom more often. We should reorganize school time and devote about one day a week to each of the following activities:

• *Independent Study.* The student, teacher, and parents should agree on an independent project, and the teacher and parents should monitor progress. Students could study a business

on-site, explore a trade, read a book, make a dress, or establish a rating guide for every public swimming pool in the area.
- *Community Service.* The student should report directly to a job in an old-age home, hospital, park, animal shelter, or other such place. The best experiences are those where the student creates a community service — training guide dogs for the blind or starting a small public garden, for example.
- *Field Curriculum.* Students should conduct large-group, teacher-led research projects in the community. For example, the class could do opinion sampling or publish a weekly price guide to supermarkets.

The two days spent in the classroom should be dedicated to tackling great themes, from what makes buildings stand up to the structure and dynamics of racial discrimination.

But reordering the school week is not enough. The most important change we can make is to set up what I call a "curriculum of family," which would serve as an umbrella over, and a foundation for, everything else.

Schools can't set up programs requiring self-discipline and self-teaching without a commitment from the home. The curriculum of family is an attitude that allows many different activities. It acknowledges that parents are the crucial factor in growing up strong and sane. If a community's places, people, procedures, and problems can become living textbooks, so can families.

Independent study, community service, and a field curriculum can't happen without permission from parents and shouldn't continue without parents being involved as partners. One way schools can promote this involvement is by asking employers to let kids visit and study their parents' workplace. They should also ask employers to free parents from their work occasionally so they can bring their experience and talent into the classroom.

Families could explore the family itself — on school time — using the sophisticated tools of ethnographers, the way Eliot Wigginton's Foxfire kids do in Rabun Gap, Georgia. This type of partnership needs institutional sanction if kids are to believe that interviewing grandmother about the craft and sociology of quilting is just as important as memorizing how a bill becomes law. Family partnerships can explore family neighborhoods and, where possible, write their own field curriculum. Undereducated, unemployed parents can come to school to do fieldwork and learn with their own children.

These are simple, inexpensive ways to use currently wasted school time and the currently wasted educational energy of parents, students, and the world to revolutionize schooling. The curriculum I've described is based on great traditions of family education in the Western World. It has been the curriculum of power for thousands of years. We have a catastrophe on our hands, and there really isn't anything to lose by trying something very different.

Why Do Bad Schools
Cost So Much?

The following address was delivered upon the occasion of Gatto's receiving the New York State Teacher of the Year Award in the summer of 1991.

I'm going to talk to you this afternoon about the mystery of why bad schools cost so much. I'm hoping to put some facts at your disposal which your experience might be able to make some sense of. What does it mean that bad schools seem to cost a fortune in the United States and that many good schools cost very little?

In Toledo, Ohio, for example, the parochial schools — which have a very good reputation — deliver a year of schooling for about $2,500 while public schools, which leave something to be desired, cost about $4,900 a seat, and the all-Ohio average for public schools is much more than $1,000 higher than that. Or here is another example: the very good private schools of Delaware have an average cost of $2,250 a year while the perfectly awful public schools there run over two-and-one-half times that figure. See how the mystery is deepening? I hope you are interested because the bill for the government schools comes out of your pocket.

The City of New York invests $7,300 a pupil, and if you are one of the people who think standardized tests measure something you'll already be aware that tests indicate only a minority of kids there can add, subtract, multiply, and divide by ninth grade. One, two, or, at best, three, of those things is all most kids can manage. Yet children who are homeschooled in that state, a group growing very rapidly, seem to read and do math years ahead of their grade level, or what would be grade level if they went to school at all. These kids cost taxpayers zero dollars and zero cents a year, which is something worth considering a little.

Finally, there is a group of kids who, despite incredible odds against them, seem to entirely educate themselves, at least for a part of their school time. We've taken to calling them "dropouts" and browbeating them as society's pariah, but an astonishing number of prominent people are drawn from their ranks. Ray Kroc, who put the zip in McDonald's, was, I believe, one of them.

The best account of self-education I ever read was the *Autobiography* of Ben Franklin, a book I'd like to see in every home for the clear simplicity with which old Ben lays down his own design for expanding the power of mind and character — using himself as a guinea pig. It seems to have worked. Don't make the common mistake of thinking Franklin lacked funds and had to make do in this fashion. He was twice enrolled in a prominent private school and twice thrown out, after which he decided he had no more time to waste on that game. Coke Stevenson, the legendary governor of Texas right up to the middle of the twentieth century and one of the sharpest legal minds west of the Pecos, had his own business running freight alone, seventy miles, on mud tracks, before he was fifteen and hardly ever saw the inside of a schoolroom.

You might be interested in knowing that in 1990 one out of every fifteen millionaires in the United States is a school dropout. I'm not trying to sell you on the idea of encouraging school dropouts necessarily, but I do want to call your attention to the fact that everything is not exactly as it seems. I want you to think for yourself what it is that makes an education instead of just believing what you are told.

These self-educating kids, like the homeschooled kids, cost the taxpayer exactly nothing. Is it possible in this age of smart bombs and fax machines to create a test that can show which kids are capable of educating themselves? I mean so that we don't stand in their way by catching them in the same net we catch the lost kids — the baffled and bewildered ones who drop out because the humiliation of staying in is too great — instead of the Franklins and Krocs and Andrew Carnegies and Coke Stevensons who drop out because they know exactly where they are going and simply lack the time to waste in school.

Well, I think there might be a way to identify these people early and overlook them for their own good if the school business stopped trying to hold on to as many bodies as possible for their dollar value. It might help, too, in clearing up general public confusion about what schooling can and can't do if school people stopped implying they possessed some magical secret that bestowed a good life on those who caught on to it and doomed the others to lifelong ignorance. Because that just isn't true. Albert Einstein didn't learn much in school according to the best accounts, and he's not the only one.

I've been a schoolteacher for almost thirty years and was just invited to be in "Who's Who In American Education." I can tell you flatly I have no secrets that Benjamin Franklin, Andrew Carnegie, Ray Kroc, Coke Stevenson, or Albert Einstein didn't have, or that half a million American families don't have from homeschooling their own kids right now. Indeed, an amazing number of folks who don't turn themselves or their kids over to professional custodians at formal schools seem to turn out better than all right.

Well, don't let me stray too far away from the subject, which is as I said, the mystery why bad schooling costs so much. I seem to have wandered into the province of whether we need schools at all, which is a topic for some other time. There is some remarkable evidence that suggests proficiency in reading, writing, and arithmetic was nearly universal at the time of the American Revolution, impossible as that is to believe now that schools fail to teach those basic skills very well in the age of the smart bomb. I know I'm still a little off the point but bear with me. In some strange way this universal literacy before we had compulsory, all-day, nearly year-round schools holds an important clue to why bad education is so expensive.

Right around the time of the Revolution the population of the colonies was approximately 2.5 million people. There were 600,000 African slaves and about 1.25 million more were indentured servants, a condition not so different from slavery during the time of the indenture. Some fraction of this non-free group consisted of children stolen right off the streets of London and Liverpool and some other towns, then dropped off on our side of the Atlantic where they were sold. I'm not telling you these things to arouse your sympathy but to draw a comparison with prospective readers today. Urban kids may be difficult to teach, but you can see that colonial America was no rose garden in that respect either.

And yet 600,000 copies of Tom Paine's lofty argument for freedom, *Common Sense,* were sold to that largely enslaved population. There's an irony there, isn't there? 600,000 copies, one for every four colonists, equivalent to a sale of 65 million books today. Of course you might think those books were bought to show off or to lay around on colonial coffee tables in the servants' quarters, but I think they were bought to read, were read, were passed to others who read them, and that they had some important hand in furnishing the upcoming Revolution with its popular philosophical justification.

Today *Common Sense* is still being read, mostly in elite colleges and graduate schools. The terms it bandies about and the somewhat intricate argument it offers require more patience and training to read than twelve years of compulsory schooling furnishes its clientele with. And yet people with no schooling at all, many of them slaves, at one time seemed to relish this kind of intellectual nourishment and call for more. Right here in this country. Imagine. Is it just barely possible that forced schooling has something to do with so many people not being able to read at all these days, or understand what they read?

On April 18, 1990 three Fordham University professors went to Boston to give a paper before the American Education Research Association Annual Meeting. The text of their contribution dealt with the mathematics of how New York City spends its public education dollars. Dull as the prose is, when Jeanne Allen, editor of *Business/Education Insider* for the Heritage Foundation sent me a copy my jaw dropped open and I began to call everyone I knew.

Why hadn't the New York papers played this on page one? Why wasn't it shouted out of every radio and television set? Well, your guess is as good as mine because even after thirty years of school-teaching I couldn't believe what I read at first. But slowly the truth of the simple numbers forced itself on me as I hope it will force itself on you:

Out of every dollar allocated to New York state schools, fifty-one percent is removed at the top for system-wide administrative costs. Local school districts remove another five percent for district administrative costs. At the school site there is wide latitude what to do with the remaining forty-four percent, but the average school deducts another twelve percent more for administration and supervision bringing the total deducted from our dollar to sixty-eight cents. But there are more nonteaching costs in most schools: coordinators of all sorts, guidance counselors, honorary administrators who are relieved of teaching duties to do favors for listed administrators. Under these flexible guidelines the thirty-two cents remaining after three administrative levies is dropped in most schools to a quarter — two bits. Out of a 7 billion dollar school budget this is a net loss to instruction from all other uses equalling 5.5 billion dollars. Think of it as protection money paid to The School Ring. Is it any wonder that the teachers who must actually spend their time confined with kids are a dispirited lot? When the gravy train pulled out they got left behind.

To appreciate the full import of this massive cash deduction from direct services for children in the New York City schools it is necessary to keep in mind that most of the student clientele would prefer not to be there, so that the money is being spent on personnel whose services are not wanted. Now you have the beginning of a way to understand why bad government schools are so expensive and even the beginning of a way to understand why they are so bad.

How did this happen? Bit-by-bit is part of the answer. Over all the twentieth century and some of the nineteenth, government schooling came to function as a jobs project and as a mechanism for contract-letting. Not all of this had to do with featherbedding and other deceptions of that sort. The changing national economy for the past one hundred years or so has made an honorable calling — honest work that has meaning — increasingly more elusive to find. With the elimination of the small farm, the small manufacturer, the hand-craftsmen, the ministry, the homemaker, teaching was seen as an infinitely elastic tent under which working people could gather to find something significant to do. Jobs and contracts became the primary mission of schools and compulsion laws guaranteed an audience no matter how bad the show. All this happened in spite of the fact that many sincere, dedicated, talented people were attracted to school work.

For a whole lot of reasons — one of them being that too many cooks spoil the broth — schools are just not set up to teach the way long experience has shown people learn. But they are set up to employ people and spend money. I remember the supervisors, and there have been many in my career, who ran around desperately trying to spend money before the fiscal clock ran down. "I don't care what you spend it on, just spend it!" I remember one man saying he had to get rid of $30,000 in a week. That was in 1972 so it would be more like $120,000 today.

No low cost solutions to the problem of schooling can possibly be seriously entertained in such a climate since all economically resourceful ideas are perceived as a threat to the existence of the system — as indeed they are. Over the years, this obsessive spending the school institution undertakes has attracted commercial and political allies who profit greatly from the business being tightly centralized, compulsory, and running exactly as it does. That is to say, from the dissatisfaction of most people. A little reflection should convince you that schools, as economic engines, are most successful when they run badly. Job tenure ensures that only personnel at the very bottom are in jeopardy in such an instance.

If this arrangement could easily be touched it would already have been hit hard by the unrelenting stream of criticism directed against our school institution for the past thirty years. Indeed, after the Secretary of Education's report in 1983, "A Nation At Risk," which warned that the nation's future was in grave peril because of the disaster in the schools, we might have expected a strong and constant light turned on these places, and swift, decisive changes. What we actually found was that the institution is impervious to criticism. However you wish to measure performance, schools are considerably worse in 1991 than they were in 1983. Administrations nationally have grown 110% since "A Nation At Risk" was issued as a whole new army of administrators emerged from the woods and leaped aboard the careening school express.

New York City is, of course, an easy corpse to kick since it has become the prime national example of how government intervention usually aggravates problems instead of solving them. A considerable number of teachers and administrators in New York are carpetbaggers, living far from the scene of their work life and sending their own children to school far from the public groves of metropolis. I'm concerned that you don't make the very common mistake, then, of thinking, "Well, that's New York, but my own school is okay, it's not one of the bad places they talk about." The truth is, I've never met anybody, not one single person, who thought there was much wrong with their school. So before I say good-bye let me tell you about Milwaukee, Wisconsin, a long way from the Atlantic island where I teach. The facts that follow are taken from the Fall 1990 issue of *Education Update:*

In beautiful Milwaukee $6,951 per student was spent last year. Central administration there skimmed off $3,481 from the top so only $2,970 actually reached the school level. Of that $2,970 only $1,647 was spent directly on instruction — just about twenty-five cents on the dollar! I think we're on to something. The New York City example apparently has a broad appeal for schoolmen everywhere, and the career tracks schooling offers are divorced from the normal risks of the marketplace.

If this system worked for kids it might be worth listening to the explanations why this money — and even more — is really "necessary," but it is a failure which seems to get worse after each and every wave of national reform. There have been about seven of those in this century. The National Association of Educational Progress says that fewer than half of all seventeen-year-olds can understand, summarize, and explain moderately complicated information. We have created a new proletariat in our government schools and we've paid through the nose for this dubious privilege.

The first thing we can do to change this sorry state of affairs is to stop believing that lack of funds invested is producing this poor performance, or that underpaid personnel are. The average private school teacher earned $17,000 in 1990 and the average government school teacher made $32,000 for a nine or ten month year. Benefits like health insurance and pension add $5-10,000 to public school compensation.

The second thing we can do is to see that certain structural aspects of compulsory public schools demand that these schools fail, irrespective of how good the teachers are. Some of these aspects are: the compulsion itself, size, irrelevant patchwork quilt curricula, bloated managements, and standardized tests. Remember the Army in Vietnam? It wasn't the best reflection on the United States, you'll agree. Now think of the Army in Iraq. One big difference between the two Armies was that the first was a drafted Army, it was there by compulsion, and the second was an all-volunteer force. According to the commander of our forces in Saudi Arabia he had less discipline problems with his 300,000 man force than he had in Vietnam commanding one thousand men. The hundreds and hundreds of types and styles of private school, religious school, homeschool, and even self-school present, in their totality, a stark contrast to compulsory government schooling — they offer real choice to families.

Before the so-called "progressive" era in this country there was a vast and impressive non-system of great diversity and autonomy in American education. No one claimed there was any one "best system" and attempted to force it on everyone. According to Lawrence Cremin, a historian of American schools, "Virtually anyone who could command a clientele could conduct classes ... Anyone could teach and anyone could learn — and the market, rather than the church or the legislature, governed through many types of contractual relationships." It was this interplay of opportunities that created the resourcefulness, the industry, and the ingenuity that President John Adams associated with the New England town and which dazzled the world. None of these schools used certified teachers, just as none of the fine American private schools like Exeter, Andover, Choate, Lawrenceville, Hill, Groton, or Collegiate do today. Teacher certification is just another expensive racket managed by The School Ring to make bad schools cost so much. Nothing magic happens in teacher colleges (quite the reverse if popular accounts are true), even though this parasitic organism, because of its monopoly on legal certification, takes in thirty percent of all college revenues nationally.

I think it must be clear which way I'm taking us, even though I'm a certified schoolteacher. Perhaps my conscience is bothering me after thirty years. We need to pry the greedy fingers of the government away from its monopoly on schooling. Let schools compete in a free market and see how long they remain as bad as they are, or as expensive. We need to stimulate the supply side and that means more than vouchers. It means underwriting promising enterprises in schooling put together by teams of entrepreneurial teachers, by parents, by businesses, by institutions, by anybody who thinks they can offer something of value. We need to give these ideas the autonomy they need for a fair trial. We need to stop being afraid of failure because that's what we already have and it is very hard to imagine anything worse. Give a portion of school taxes back to parents who want to shop around the old and new options for a better deal than they are getting. That's not only a sounder way to run the school thing, it is the original American way. Time to come home to ourselves, time to listen to our own best genius.

A Year With John Taylor Gatto

The following letter was originally written for publication in the Children's Express Quarterly. *It was written by a 13-year-old student, Jamaal M. Watson.*

Mr. Gatto is always saying to us that the idea of some stranger teaching you anything is just a scam. The only person who ever teaches you anything is yourself.

Each of us has a one-of-a-kind identity — just as we all have one-of-a-kind fingerprints — and what education means is to develop that unique personality so that we each know who we are. Self-discovery is at the bottom of being somebody real. Most kids imitate what they see on TV and do what the teacher tells them to do, but you can't become real that way.

To discover yourself and find your path through life, you need to have lots of firsthand experiences, mostly on your own in tough situations. It doesn't do much good to get these experiences second hand from books.

The way Mr. Gatto likes the Lab School to work is that every kid gets six different kinds of experience. First and most important is independent study, a day out of the school building alone or with a friend, going anywhere we want to go and studying anything we want to study. The best kind of independent study is when you have one big idea, for instance, you want to find all the ways that the ancient Greeks, Romans and Egyptians still influence New

York City, and you break that idea into parts — architecture, law, clothing, etc. — and you hunt for answers for a whole year. That way each day builds toward something big that's all your own.

A lot of kids can't do that so they might have five or ten projects in a year, and that's okay, too. Whatever works for you is right, and only you can know what that is. Mr. Gatto doesn't offer any help unless you ask him for it.

The second kind of experience is apprenticeships. I'm apprenticed to an Editor at the *West Side Spirit* newspaper, Nubia is apprenticed to State Senator Paterson, Tuwan is a guide at the Transit Museum. What you learn in an apprenticeship is how someone thinks when they are doing their work, how they make decisions, what they look out for.

The third kind of experience is community service. We spend one full day a week helping others, not being a parasite — for a change. Some of our kids serve at a homeless shelter, one entertains in old people's homes . . . things like that.

Notice there's only two days left of the school week?!

Some days we're teamed up with our own parents or somebody else's to do Family Teamwork Curriculum. Maybe I'd spend the day on my father's job, or plant flowerpots with my mother, or paint a room with my uncle, or read to my grandmother. The idea is to recognize that your family is the most important thing you'll ever be part of.

The last kind of experience is "class" work. Mr. Gatto hates the idea we are numbered, graded and locked up with people our same age, and he hates the idea we have to move like laboratory rats when a bell rings.

But because we have to be there, what he does with the classroom time is to give us practice exercises in thinking. We analyze everything and anything, and we even practice "dialectics," which is thinking where you just automatically assume that anything an authority tells you is dead wrong. Then you work to find out whether it is dead wrong, or really right.

You should know that anytime Mr. Gatto or one of us sees an opportunity on any given day to do something more important than what was planned, we have a right to make substitutions.

You should also know that the school doesn't make things easy for us. (Mr. Gatto directs an alternative program called the "Lab" within a regular public junior high school.) Everybody bad mouths us behind our backs. Our room is battered and beaten because so many other classes use it who don't respect our property. We never use textbooks but instead xerox all our reading materials, but the school has forbidden us to use the photocopy machine! And we need to travel all around the city on a minute's notice, but the school says we can't go unless we give two weeks advance notice. Do we cheat and sneak out anyway? I'll let you guess.

In my own year and a half in the Lab, I've won two citywide essay contests, been on TV four or five times, gotten a long-term apprenticeship with Annie Nocente, the Marvel Comic Book creator of *Daredevil*, visited twenty-two engineering sites in New York and New Jersey, and have gotten a part in a movie about schools . . . even though I'm only thirteen. And I was accepted to a famous art high school for the fall.

Mr. Gatto helped me see that I really am my own best teacher.

We Can't Afford School Reform

This address was delivered on November 2, 1990, on the occasion of Mr. Gatto being named New York City Teacher of the Year for the second consecutive year, by the New York Alliance for Public Schools. The award ceremony took place in the ballroom of the Hotel Inter-Continental in Manhattan.

Mayor Dinkins, Chancellor Fernandez, Members of the Alliance, thank you for this honor.

And thank you for choosing this lovely space to confer it in. Where we conduct our affairs shows how serious we really are about things, I think. I wish I could say I was reminded of the schoolrooms I've taught in the for past thirty years. But I can't say that.

Rooms speak bluntly; they tell the truth. This room says that life has graceful moments. It allows plain people like myself to be transformed by their surroundings. There aren't any rooms like this in my school. Schoolrooms speak a different message. I want to translate their language for you.

Let me begin by talking about some fine teachers: three kids I work with who went this morning to a different kind of schoolroom, a basement kitchen in the Presbyterian Church on 114th Street and Broadway. Every Friday morning, they go there to chop potatoes and carrots, stir banana pudding, cut bread, fill bowls with peanut butter, wash dishes, and set places at table in preparation for the arrival of 240 homeless men, women, children, and babies. When their job is done the room is filled with food and good will. For the next three hours they serve the food to hungry people who don't have rooms to live in, people whose bedroom and schoolroom is often the great outdoors.

These kids have names: Derrick Graham, Michael Pettway and Gerald Matthews. Just yesterday I heard a teacher call Derrick "rude and abusive" and the same day I heard someone else put Gerald down in similar fashion, but whatever the school system thinks of Derrick, Michael and Gerald, to the homeless they look like angels and work like demons.

By working hard feeding needy men and women these boys become amazing self-teachers, teaching themselves discipline, obligation, organization, and many other attributes of educated men. Instead of consorting with children all day in schoolrooms they work shoulder to shoulder with Columbia University students — and that seems to make a difference in how they respond.

While they work, Derrick, Mike, and Gerald learn food preparation, planning ahead, economy, how to set a table, how to serve a four-course meal, and how to clean up afterwards in preparation for the next round. Maybe in the future one of them will make a fortune as a restaurateur because of this, maybe one of them will open a soup kitchen. Whatever may connect with this work, nobody could deny the boys are getting an important part of an education in that church basement on 114th Street. Even though they miss "school" to do it.

The junior high school where I teach might offer some of the same opportunities to educate that the soup kitchen does if its great rooms — like the boiler room, the cafeteria, or the principal's office — were freed up to educate with. But that would take an act of the legislature, a ruling by the Chancellor, a decision by the District Superintendent, a commitment by the building principal, a green light from the teacher's union, an approval in writing from the parents association, good cooperation from all other levels of authority, and the blessing of the custodian.

No, I'm afraid my school couldn't help the homeless. By the time we got all those people to agree someone would have died and we'd have to start all over from the beginning.

The best evidence that our schools are set up to "school" and not be useful educationally lies in the look of the rooms where we confine kids. Rooms with no clocks or mirrors, no telephones, no fax machines, no stamps, no envelopes, no maps, no directories, no private space in which to think, no conference tables on which to confer. Rooms in which there isn't any real way to contact the outside world where life is going on.

To get where real life is a kid needs a pass from his home room teacher, his subject teacher, his mother, his guidance counselor, his grade advisor, and his building principal. By the time he got all those passes something would have died.

Schoolrooms speak bluntly all right; they tell the truth. The rooms my daughter Briseis worked in as a math teacher at Martin Luther King High School didn't even have windows. That was someone's idea of the proper place for kids from Harlem — in windowless rooms. The last rooms Briseis saw as a teacher — before she quit in disgust — had only walls and a door, no windows. The ventilation system was broken all that last year. She quit when she heard they were planning to take off the doors.

Schoolrooms tell the truth of what the school business is really up to. It's something important but not something anybody in his right mind would call education.

What is it then?

If anyone intends to change schools he needs first to grit his teeth and face the fact schools work very well just as they are. They work exactly the way they were intended to work by the great schoolmen who fashioned compulsory schooling: Plato, Erasmus, Bacon, Horace Mann, Chancellor von Bismarck, E. L. Thorndyke, and all the rest. That's not to say these places work as you or I might want them to work, but they do the job they were supposed to do.

What schools are about in their structural design is dependency, obedience, regulation, and the subordination an orderly class system needs — in which people stick to their own kind and don't get out of line. Schools achieve these goals by endless exercises in subordination.

A simple way to look at it is schools teach you to stay in the room to which you have been assigned. Schools establish and maintain a class system although that's not what America is supposed to be about.

Schools make childhood surreal by the application of Kafka-like rituals:

- They enforce sensory deprivation on classes of children held in featureless, sometimes windowless rooms.
- They sort children into rigid categories by the use of fantastic measures like age-grading, or standardized test scores.

- They train children to drop whatever they are occupied with and to move as a body from room to room at the sound of bell, buzzer, horn or klaxon.
- They keep children under constant surveillance, depriving them of private time and space.
- They assign children numbers constantly, feigning the ability to discriminate qualities quantitatively.
- They insist that every moment of time be filled with low-level abstractions, even reaching into the private sanctuaries of home with a tool called "homework."
- They forbid children their own discoveries, pretending to possess some vital secret which children must surrender their active learning time to acquire.

We pay a heavy price for confining young people to schoolrooms, as those of you who read newspapers or watch television will be aware. Although the children I teach look, sound, and move much like children in any past era, you should not be misled by surface similarity. By and large my kids are indifferent to the past, indifferent to the future, indifferent to each other, and indifferent to themselves. They don't seem to be able to hold interest in anything for very long.

You don't suppose there might be some connection between those bells, buzzers, horns and klaxons summoning them to another room every forty minutes and this massive indifference to things, do you? Think about it. Schools teach that nothing is very important — certainly nothing is important enough to spend more than forty minutes on at any one time.

Among things you need to know about the kids I see is that

they don't like themselves very much. I'm not surprised. In school-rooms people are useless. Schoolrooms are like an engine without a driveshaft. They burn up a lot of energy running but the power is useless. Useless people seldom like themselves very much. The children we capture sense the time they are losing is precious time, time that will never return. They dislike themselves for not know-ing how to save their lives and turn time to real use.

A lot of my kids don't like their families very much either. One of our eighth graders murdered his parents last May for the insur-ance money. He was thirteen or fourteen (and there wasn't any in-surance money) but he saw a murder like that on television and figured everyone had insurance who wasn't a kid. That's an awful thing to say but this disaffection of families is built into the way we school — shutting parents out of the important rooms of their own kids' lives.

No effect of compulsory mass-schooling is more resistant to remedy than the damage it has done to the American family by separating parents and kids. If teachers claim privileged in-formation about education, and school-time takes the best time available for the self-discoveries of growing up, then the most im-portant reason for families to exist at all vanishes. Families are ru-ined. The worst ruined are the ones who keep their children under surveillance, and report any deviance to school authorities. Par-ents regularly betray their children to school people because of invisible assumptions they never examine.

Schoolrooms as we've designed them have no place for par-ents, and in the room-like sets of television we have replaced fam-ily myths with dishonest stories told by actors — men and women who pretend to be people they are not. Sometimes they pretend to murder relatives for insurance money but always they are pretending something. And you and I pretend that all this is harmless.

In between the myths of schooling and the myths of television, a priesthood of pitchmen replaces family magic with magical products and magical services that pretend to do magical things that they cannot. Love is often measured by how many of these things a family can buy. Is it any wonder that a lot of my kids dislike their families who can't buy them much?

What prevents school reform from happening isn't bad people, I think, but a strange economy that renders many lives absurd. We don't want to face that because it scares us, and it should. It's just easier to talk about engineering solutions to the school problem, solutions that common sense and hard work can bring about. I prefer that myself.

If you think about it, it's impossible not to be frightened by the damage that would follow if schooling took place in important rooms that transformed the people in them, as law courts and corporate boardrooms do — important rooms like family living rooms, and places where parents work, hospitals, nurseries, or rooms like the room where my kids serve food to homeless men. What would happen to all the real estate we call school?

Think of the economic tragedy that would occur if schools taught critical thinking. If they encouraged individuals to be strong and to think original thoughts. If they taught the philosopher's secret that nothing important can be bought. If they honored the universal human need for choice and privacy. If they nourished a love of quality. Who would crave the mountains of junk our mass-production economy distributes? Who would eat the processed food? Who would wear the plastic shoes? Who would fill evenings with televised fantasies in place of living? How could the mass economy survive without the training "schools" provide? We'll never get a handle on school reform until we understand this strange symbiosis better.

Ernest Boyer of the Carnegie Foundation says conditions in schools have gotten worse, not better, behind the cloud of reform rhetoric of the past few years. I don't know a single teacher who wouldn't agree. It's more than just a matter of rolling up our sleeves and trying harder.

We have to face the frustrating fact that reform cannot avoid hurting a lot of people and a lot of powerful interests if it succeeds, people who have worked long and hard and, yes, honorably, to get into a position to sell us the kind of schools we don't need. They aren't bad people or bad companies, just irrelevant, out of place, in the way. Reform of schools has never succeeded partly because of this failure to recognize the inevitability of resistance on the part of those threatened by change. No strategy that expects the simple power of reason or engineering solutions to prevail is ever going to work because many livelihoods and much power has to be threatened in order to stop schooling and start educating.

Another unpleasant reality reformers prefer not to face is the invisible secondary function of the school institution as a jobs-project for grownups and a renewable patronage resource for local politicians. It wasn't lunacy that created all those useless jobs at Central Board, and in every one of the Community School Boards, or in most of the individual schools. It was natural self-interest and also a natural human inclination to take care of cousins and friends, or to trade favors. Politicians have always done that and will apparently keep on doing it no matter how much outrage we generate.

Just suppose we could have a magic wand and clear out all the thousands and thousands of superfluous people in the schools tomorrow? Suppose we could do that and turn the resources they waste into positive things for children? What on earth would happen to all those people we throw out? Where would they go? Would my children end up feeding them at the Broadway soup kitchen?

You see what's wrong with the habit of magical thinking that schools and television teach — it leads to a way of looking at problems that is just too narrow. The things I've named are parts of the school reform question that go undiscussed, in public at least. People prefer to talk about engineering solutions. Surely that's an important part of the reason we're stuck, unable to fix the school mess, even though we increasingly realize the school institution is bleeding off our vitality as a nation.

I'll conclude these remarks by suggesting some roads to travel to find better schools that needn't cost us an extra cent, roads that are easy to follow, which lead to a better destination for kids — education in place of schooling. I'll give you an outline of an engineering solution as I see it, keeping in mind that my ideas are of limited utility without a political solution, and that no political solution will stick unless it's democratically derived and expresses the will of all the people. If experts could have fixed our schools the schools would be fixed by now. Top-down solutions won't play any more, bottom-up ones are what we need.

In the first place, teaching needs to be de-constructed as a job with bosses and reconstructed as professions are: entrepreneurial, with large amounts of autonomy. Let the free market decide good schools and good teachers. And teachers themselves need to be centrally involved in the development and maintenance of standards of practice. They need to be architects, not the workmen for someone else's blueprint.

Kids and their families need tremendous amounts of pure choice in the way they come to the problem of growing up. There is no "one right way" to do it, there never was. I don't think we'll see any great improvement in schools until centralized government is willing to release its chokehold on what is possible. And the phenomenal successes of homeschooling show at least one possibility that needs to be encouraged. There are others, too, of course.

The great structures of schooling — time, place, personnel, curriculum — need a severe rethinking. Take personnel. Too many people we tab as teachers are picked green from their own extended childhoods. Fresh from college, without sufficient or significant life-tests, they are placed in hothouse classrooms to ripen, broken from the natural environment in which men and women mature, through struggle, adventure, experiment, risk-taking, and plenty of independent choices.

Instead of staffing the business with college graduates of recent vintage because they are cheap and tractable, I would make it a profession open largely to mature men and women who have proven themselves worthy of teaching others. My guess is that the inherent attractiveness of pedagogy would draw a good share of the best seasoned people to an enterprise so conceived. I think they would be challenged by work so significant, and experienced people have inherent advantages in understanding the value of work that isn't absurd.

We need strategies for getting beyond the orthodox in space and time management. For example, the role of privacy and solitude in character development, and mental development, too, has been grossly neglected by our form of schooling. Schools are too big by a factor of ten or twenty. What is needed are hundreds of thousands of intimate, *ad hoc* facilities — park benches, rooftops, river banks, living rooms, places of business.

Large schools aren't set up to work. They deny flexible time and appropriate space for anyone to do real work in, and that includes teachers. When multiple gatekeepers must be approached to do the smallest task, like making a phone call or getting a paper clip, then work soon is deliberately avoided. We need to trust each other, because policing is too expensive and it makes us all crazy

As for curriculum, the place of the part in the whole is lost when things of the mind are broken into artificial subject divisions using a Henry Ford assembly-line philosophy. The problems of the real world are interdisciplinary, the problems assigned by schools should be, too, in large part.

Finally; a study of any list of great men and women will quickly disclose the host of personal methods they used to arrive at personal enlightenment — an education. No one I know ever gave much credit to the daily doses of abstraction prescribed by strangers and imposed on his life by compulsion. But plenty of autobiographies credit a mother, a father, a grandmother, a grandfather, an uncle, an aunt, or a chance accident happened upon while adventuring. Maybe there's a lesson there.

Nothing worthwhile is learned by compulsion. Surely we've

grown up enough as a country to understand that by now.

Once again, thank you for the honor. I've enjoyed the chance to speak to you in this pretty room today.

Part Two
Analyzing the System

Universal Education

Let's get it clear in our minds that schooling is not education — you can easily compensate for lacking a schooling, but there is no way to make up for the damage that occurs without an education. Without that you are smaller than you would have been.

Plenty of brilliant and famous people have lacked schooling — George Washington, Benjamin Franklin, Admiral Farragut, Thomas Edison, Margaret Meade, and many more — but all of them had a fine education.

Schooling takes place in an environment controlled by others, through procedures and sequences more or less controlled by others, and for the purposes of others. There's a value to this when the teachers are people who care for you and struggle to understand you, but even then schooling is never enough.

Education describes efforts largely self-initiated for the purpose of taking charge of your life wisely and living in a world you understand. The educated state is a complex tapestry woven out of broad experience, grueling commitments, and substantial risk-taking.

In our own society, schooling can help or hinder learning, encourage or discourage education.

Let me tell you about Stanley, a young man I met while teaching in New York City. Stanley only came to school one day a month and got away with it because I was his home room teacher, and I covered for him. I didn't do it to be a lawbreaker, but because Stanley explained to me where he was spending his time, and I agreed with him that it was more educational than what went on in school.

It seems Stanley had five aunts and uncles — all in business for themselves before they were twenty-one — and he wanted to follow in their footsteps. One was a florist, one an unfinished furniture builder, one a deli owner, one had a little restaurant, and one owned a delivery service. What Stanley did when he cut school was to work for no pay for all these uncles and aunts, one after another. He was passed from store to store doing free labor in exchange for the opportunity to learn the business.

"Hey Mr. Gatto," he said to me, "this way I get a chance to decide what business I want for myself. You tell me what books to read, I'll read them, but I don't have time to waste in school unless I want to end up like the rest of you — working for somebody else."

After I heard that I couldn't in good conscience keep him locked up. Could you?

Education for the Masses

The secret of American schooling is not that it doesn't teach the way children learn. It's that it isn't supposed to teach about being a strong, self-directed man or woman — something Stanley had taken upon himself to learn on his own.

School was engineered to serve a modified command economy and an increasingly layered social order. It wasn't made for the benefit of kids and families, as those people would define their own needs. School is the first impression children get of organized society. Like most first impressions, it lasts.

The dynamics that make modern schooling poisonous to healthy human development aren't difficult to spot: the work in classrooms isn't significant work; it fails to satisfy real needs pressing on the individual; it doesn't answer real questions experience raises in the young mind; it doesn't contribute to solving problems encountered in actual life. The net effect of making all work external to individual longings, experiences, questions, and problems is to render the victim listless.

This phenomenon has been well understood at least since the time of the British enclosure movement, which forced small farmers off their land into factory work. Growth and mastery come to those who vigorously self-direct. Initiating, creating, doing, being alone, reflecting, free associating — these are precisely what schooling is set up to prevent.

Schools train individuals to respond as a mass. Boys and girls are drilled in being bored, frightened, envious, emotionally needy, generally incomplete. A successful mass production economy requires such a clientele. Small business and small farm economies, like those of the Amish, require individual competence, thoughtfulness, compassion, and universal participation. Our own economy requires a managed mass of levelled, spiritless, anxious, family-less, friendless, godless, and obedient people who believe the difference between Coke and Pepsi is a subject worth arguing about.

The extreme wealth of American big business is a direct result of school training in certain attitudes, such as a craving for novelty. That's what the bells are for. They don't ring so much as say, "And now for something different, thank God."

The History of Scientific Schooling

Between 1896 and 1920, a small group of industrialists and financiers, together with their private charitable foundations, subsidized university chairs and researchers, and school administrators, spent more money on schooling than the government itself did, with the aim of bending schooling to the service of business and the political state. Carnegie and Rockefeller alone, as late as 1915, were spending more than the state. In this laissez-faire fashion, a system of modern schooling was constructed without public participation.

The motives for this involvement were undoubtedly mixed, but it will be useful to read this excerpt from the first mission statement of Rockefeller's General Education Board, from a document called "Occasional Letter Number One":

> "In our dreams . . . people yield themselves with perfect docility to our molding hands. The present education conventions fade from their minds, and unhampered by tradition we work our own goodwill upon a grateful and responsive folk.
>
> "We shall not try to make these people or any of their children into philosophers or men of learning or men of science. We have not to raise up from them authors, educators, poets, or men of letters. We shall not search for embryo great artists, painters, musicians, nor lawyers, doctors, preachers, politicians, statesmen, of whom we have an ample supply.
>
> "The task is simple. We will organize children and

teach them in a perfect way the things their fathers and mothers are doing in an imperfect way."

Another insider of modern schooling, H. H. Goddard, chair of psychology at Princeton, said in 1920 that government schooling is "the perfect organization of the hive." He wrote that standardized testing would cause the lower classes to face their biological inferiority (sort of like wearing a public dunce cap), which would discourage their reproduction.

The NEA in 1930 sharpened our understanding by specifying in a resolution of its Department of Superintendence that what was being served was an "effective use of capital" through which our "unprecedented wealth-producing power has been gained."

School is best seen as the critical terminal on a production line to create a utopia resembling Epcot Center, but with one important limitation: it isn't intended for everyone.

Out of Johns Hopkins in 1996 came this chilling news: the American economy has grown massively since the mid-1960s, but workers' real, spendable wages are no higher than they were thirty years ago.

That's from the book *Fat and Mean* by David Gordon about the significance of corporate downsizing. During the boom economy of the 1980s and 1990s, purchasing power rose for twenty percent of the population and actually declined about thirteen percent for the other eighty percent. Indeed, after inflation is factored in, purchasing power of a working *couple* in 1995 is only eight percent greater than for a *single* workingman in 1905. This steep decline in common prosperity over ninety years has forced both parents from many homes and deposited their kids in the management systems of daycare and extended schooling.

Despite the century-long harangue that schooling is the cure for unevenly spread wealth, exactly the reverse has occurred — wealth is 250 percent more concentrated at century's end than it was at its beginning.

What Private School Parents Want

Now that we know what forced public schooling is intended to do for the lower classes, let's take a look at what parents at the finest private schools want from schooling. I've been studying their expectations for nearly twenty years in order to compare them with my own goals. I'm talking about the twenty ritziest private boarding schools in America — schools like Groton, St. Paul's, Deerfield, and Kent.

I'm going to ask you to note that none of the principles these parents seek cost a penny to develop. Everybody could do one or all these things with their kids just as well as Exeter or St. Paul's could. What these elite private school parents want schools to teach their children, in no particular order of importance, are:

- Good manners and the ability to display those manners to everyone without thinking, because they know in this way their children will be welcome everywhere.
- Hard intellectual knowledge, undiluted, but in simple English so no specialized jargon interferes with understanding the fundamental ideas.
- Love and appreciation for the land and the natural world of

plants and animals, because without this understanding, life becomes lonely, barren, and abstract.

• A public sense of decorum so that they can adapt naturally to every setting they find themselves in without provoking anger and opposition.

• A common core of western culture so that all the generations can be comfortable with a shared set of tastes and values.

• Leadership; they aren't interested in their children being part of a managed herd.

• Self-discipline.

A major concern of private school parents is that the schools understand the partially invisible qualification system that provides access to key positions in the economy. These parents expect schools to qualify their children to move freely through the economic system. But don't we all want this?

Private school parents also demand individualized attention for their children, small classes, continuous pressure on their children to stretch individual limits, exposure to many different theoretical and practical aspects of life, and exercises to develop self-reliance and self-confidence.

To be educated is to understand yourself and others, to know your culture and that of others, your history and that of others, your religious outlook and that of others. If you miss out on this, you are always at the mercy of someone else to interpret what the facts of any situation mean.

The Amish

Now let me tell you something about the Old Order Amish, a group of 150,000 very prosperous people who came to America with little more than the clothes on their backs. Everyone's heard about the Amish, but few people know the astonishing details. Here they are:

- Virtually every adult Amisher has an independent livelihood as the owner of a farm or a business.
- There is almost no crime, no violence, no alcoholism, no divorce, and no drug-taking in the group.
- They accept no government help with health care, old-age assistance, or schooling after eighth grade. (They were forced by the government to accept first through eighth-grade schooling.)
- The success rate of Amish in small business is ninety-five percent compared to the national rate in the U.S. of fifteen percent.
- All Amish children have a chance to take a sabbatical year away from Amish life when they arrive at the verge of adulthood to decide if they want to remain in the community and meet its customs. Eighty-five percent of all grown children prefer to remain in the community — a principal reason the group has grown 3000 percent in the twentieth century.

Almost all members, when interviewed by outside investigators, report satisfaction with their lives. Donald Kraybill of Johns Hopkins University studied a thousand Amish businesses for a book published in 1995 called *Amish Enterprise*. He had this to say:

"[The Amish] challenge a lot of conventional assumptions about what it takes to enter business. They don't have high school educations; they don't have specialized training; they don't use computers; they don't use electricity or automobiles; they don't have training in how to create a marketing plan.

"But the resources they transfer over from the farm are: an entrepreneurial spirit, a willingness to take risks, innovativeness, a strong work ethic, a cheap family labor pool and high standards of craftsmanship. One of their values is smallness. They don't want their shops and industries to get large. This spreads entrepreneurship widely across the whole settlement."

This also is a big part of the Amish definition of education. I'll add a little more:

The Amish are legendary good neighbors, first to volunteer in times of outer-world need. They open their farms to ghetto children and frequently rear handicapped children from the non-Amish world whom nobody else wants. They farm so well and so profitably without using tractors, chemical fertilizers, or pesticides, that Mexico, Canada, Russia, France, and Uruguay have hired them as advisors on raising agricultural productivity.

You can figure out a lot about what the Amish believe an education is from the things they fought the government about — and won — when the Supreme Court ruled they had to go to school from first through eighth grade.

The Amish realized the new government schools were social separators built on the principle of mechanical milk separators, whirling the young mind about until both the social structure of the parents and the coherent consciousness are fragmented. Schooling separates people from the daily content of life, dividing the world into disciplines, courses, classes, grades, and teachers who remain strangers to their children in all but name. Even religion is studied, analyzed, and eventually separated from family, history, and daily life. It became just another subject for critical analysis.

And the constant competition would destroy many, leaving a multitude of losers, humiliated and self-hating — a far cry from the universal strength Amish community life requires. The Amish wanted no part of that. They demanded that:

- Schools be located within walking distance of home.
- There be no large schools where pupils are sorted into compartments and assigned different teachers each year.
- School decisions be under parents' control.
- The school year be no longer than eight months.
- Teachers be knowledgeable in and sympathetic with Amish values and rural ways.
- Their children be taught that wisdom and academic knowledge are two different commodities.
- Every kid have practical internships and apprenticeships supervised by parents.

Education for Unique People

What can we learn from Stanley, the private school parents, and the Amish? We hear endless talk about school reform, but real school reform would have to defeat the belief that any such reality as "mass man" actually exists. We would have to believe instead what our fingerprints and our intuition tell us — no two people are alike, nobody can be accurately profiled by numbers and graphs.

To have a kind of education that served individuals, families, and communities we would need to abandon forever the notion — learned in school and reinforced through every institution — that ordinary people are too stupid, too irresponsible, too childish to look out for ourselves.

We need to admit finally that knowledge is a useful thing but that it is a far cry from wisdom, and without wisdom we wander like lost sheep. We need to honor our founding documents and founding ideas, to acknowledge that each of us has the right to live as we deem wise. And if the way we choose means disaster for global corporations — as the way of the Amish embraced by too many surely would — then that fateful choice must still be honored.

I want to leave you on a hopeful note. We have ample evidence from the experiment of American history that ordinary people, trusted to be sovereign, can do extraordinary things. We have abundant examples around us in the form of determined groups like the Amish and determined individuals like Stanley that despite a discouraging political climate for writing one's own script, it is still possible to do so. Only a little courage is needed. I wish you that courage. We shall change this thing in time if we deny it our cooperation, affirming what our hearts and history tell us is true.

Confederacy of Dunces: The Tyranny of Compulsory Schooling

Let me speak to you about dumbness because that is what schools teach best. Old-fashioned dumbness used to be simple ignorance: you didn't know something, but there were ways to find out if you wanted to. Compulsory schooling didn't eliminate dumbness — in fact, we now know that people read more fluently before we had forced schooling — but dumbness was transformed.

Now dumb people aren't just ignorant; they're the victims of non-thought-of secondhand ideas. Dumb people are now well-informed about the opinions of *Time* magazine and CBS, *The New York Times* and the President; their job is to choose which pre-thought thoughts, which received opinions, they like best. The elite in this new empire of ignorance are those who know the most pre-thought thoughts.

Mass dumbness is vital to modern society. The dumb person is wonderfully flexible clay for psychological shaping by market research, government policymakers, public-opinion leaders, and any other interest group. The more pre-thought thoughts a person has memorized, the easier it is to predict what choices he or she will make. What dumb people cannot do is think for themselves or ever be alone for very long without feeling crazy. That is the whole point of national forced schooling; we aren't supposed to be able to think for ourselves because independent thinking gets in the way of "professional" thinking, which is believed to follow rules of scientific precision.

Modern scientific stupidity masquerades as intellectual knowledge — which it is not. Real knowledge has to be earned by hard and painful thinking; it can't be generated in group discussions or group therapies but only in lonely sessions with yourself. Real knowledge is earned only by ceaseless questioning of yourself and others, and by the labor of independent verification. You can't buy it from a social worker, a psychologist, a licensed specialist, or a schoolteacher. There isn't a public school in this country set up to allow the discovery of real knowledge — not even the best ones — although here and there individual teachers, like guerrilla fighters, sabotage the system and work toward this ideal. But since schools are set up to classify people rather than to see them as unique, even the best schoolteachers are strictly limited in the amount of questioning they can tolerate.

The new dumbness — the non-thought-of received ideas — is much more dangerous than simple ignorance, because it's really about thought control. In school, a washing away of the innate power of individual mind takes place, a cleansing so comprehensive that original thinking becomes difficult. If you don't believe this development was part of the intentional design of schooling, you should read William Torrey Harris's *The Philosophy of Education*. Harris was the U.S. Commissioner of Education at the turn of the century and the man most influential in standardizing our schools. Listen to the man.

"Ninety-nine [students] out of a hundred," writes Harris, "are automata, careful to walk in prescribed paths, careful to follow the prescribed custom." This is not an accident, Harris explains, but the "result of substantial education, which, scientifically defined, is the subsumption of the individual."

Scientific education subsumes the individual until his or her behavior becomes robotic. Those are the thoughts of the most influential U.S. Commissioner of Education we've had so far.

The great theological scholar Dietrich Bonhoeffer raised this issue of the new dumbness in his brilliant analysis of Nazism, in which he sought to comprehend how the best-schooled nation in the world, Germany, could fall under its sway. He concluded that Nazism could be understood only as the psychological product of good schooling. The sheer weight of received ideas, pre-thought thoughts, was so overwhelming that individuals gave up trying to assess things for themselves. Why struggle to invent a map of the world or of the human conscience when schools and media offer thousands of ready-made maps, pre-thought thoughts?

The new dumbness is particularly deadly to middle and upper-middle class people, who have already been made shallow by the multiple requirements to conform. Too many people, uneasily convinced that they must know something because of a degree, diploma, or license, remain so convinced until a brutal divorce, alienation from their children, loss of employment, or periodic fits of meaninglessness manage to tip the precarious mental balance of their incomplete humanity.

Listen to William Harris again, the dark genius of American schooling, the man who gave you scientifically age-graded classrooms:

"The great purposes of school can be realized
better in dark, airless, ugly places than in beautiful halls.
It is to master the physical self, to transcend the beauty

of nature. School should develop the power to withdraw from the external world."

Harris thought, a hundred years ago, that self-alienation was the key to a successful society. Filling the young mind with the thoughts of others and surrounding it with ugliness — that was the passport to self-alienation. Who can say that he was wrong?

I want to give you a yardstick, a gold standard, by which to measure good schooling. The Shelter Institute in Bath, Maine will teach you how to build a three thousand square-foot, multi-level Cape Cod home in three weeks' time, whatever your age. If you stay another week, it will show you how to make your own posts and beams; you'll actually cut them out and set them up. You'll learn wiring, plumbing, insulation, the works. Twenty thousand people have learned how to build a house there for about the cost of one month's tuition in public school. For just about the same money you can walk down the street in Bath to the Apprentice Shop at the Maine Maritime Museum and sign on for a one-year course (no vacations, forty hours a week) in traditional wooden boat building. The whole tuition is eight hundred dollars, but there's a catch: they won't accept you as a student until you volunteer for two weeks, so they can get to know you and you can judge what it is you're getting into. Now you've invested thirteen months and fifteen hundred dollars and you have a house and a boat. What else would you like to know? How to grow food, make clothes, repair a car, build furniture, sing? Those of you with a historical imagination will recognize Thomas Jefferson's prayer for schooling — that it would teach useful knowledge. Some places do: the best schooling in the United States today is coming out of museums, libraries, and private institutes. If anyone wants to school your kids, hold them to the standard of the Shelter Institute and you'll do fine.

As long as we're questioning public schooling, we should question whether there really is an abstraction called "the public" at all, except in the calculations of social engineers. As a boy from the banks of the Monongahela River in western Pennsylvania, I find the term a cartoon of social reality. If an institution that deprives people of their right to self-determination can call itself "public"; if the state can take your home because you can't pay its "public" school taxes, and state courts can break up your family if you refuse to allow the state to school your children — then the word public is a label for institutions that allow people to be treated like slaves.

A few weeks is all that the Shelter Institute asks for to give you a beautiful Cape Cod home; a few months is all Maine Maritime asks for to teach you boat-building and rope-making, sail-making, fishing and naval architecture. We have too much schooling, not too little. Hong Kong, with its short school year, whips Japan in every scientific or mathematical competition. Israel, with its long school year, can't keep up with Flemish Belgium, which has the shortest school year in the world.

Somebody's been lying to you. Sweden, a rich, healthy, and beautiful country with a spectacular reputation for quality in everything won't allow children to enter school before they're seven years old. The total length of Swedish schooling is nine years, not twelve, after which the average Swede runs circles around the over-schooled American. Why don't you know these things? To whose advantage is it that you don't?

When students enroll in a Swedish school, the authorities ask three questions: (1) Why do you want to go to this school? (2) What do you want to gain from the experience? (3) What are you interested in?

And they listen to the answers.

How did I survive for nearly thirty years in a system for which I feel such loathing? I want to make a confession in the hope it will suggest strategy to other teachers: I did it by becoming an active saboteur, in small ways and large. What I did resolutely was to teach kids what I'm saying here — that schooling is bad business unless it teaches you how to build a boat or a house; that giving strangers intimate information about yourself is certainly to their advantage, but seldom to your own.

On a daily basis I consciously practiced sabotage, breaking laws regularly, forcing the fixed times and spaces of schooling to become elastic, falsifying records so the rigid curricula of those places could be what individual children needed. I threw sand in the gears by encouraging new teachers to think dialectically so that they wouldn't fit into the pyramid of administration. I exploited the weakness of the school's punitive mechanism, which depends on fear to be effective, by challenging it in visible ways, showing I did not fear it, setting administrators against each other to prevent the juggernaut from crushing me. When that didn't work I recruited community forces to challenge the school — businessmen, politicians, parents, and journalists — so I would be given a wide berth. Once, under heavy assault, I asked my wife to run for school board. She got elected, fired the superintendent, and then punished his cronies in a host of imaginative ways.

But what I am most proud of is this: I undermined the confidence of the young in the school institution and replaced it with confidence in their own minds and hearts. I thumbed my nose at William Torrey Harris and gave to my children (although I was well into manhood before I shook off the effects of my own schooling) what had been given to me by the green river Monongahela and the steel city of Pittsburgh: love of family, friends, culture, and neighborhood, and a cup overflowing with self-respect. I taught my kids how to cheat destiny so successfully that they created a record of astonishing success that deserves a book someday. Some of my kids left school to go up the Amazon and live with Indian tribes to study on their own the effects of government dam-building on traditional family life; some went to Nicaragua and joined combat teams to study the amazing hold of poetry on the lives of common people in that land; some made award-winning movies; some became comedians; some succeeded at love, some failed. All learned to argue with Fate in the form of social engineering.

I hope you saw the news story a while back about a national milk price-rigging scheme in schools from Florida to Utah. Fifty-six arrests have already been made in a caper that's existed most of this century. Schools pay more for milk than any other bulk buyer. Does that surprise you? Ask your own school administrator what unit price he pays for school milk and he'll look at you like your marbles are gone. How should he know, why should he care? An assistant principal once said to me, "It's not *your* money. What are you getting excited about?"

What if I told you that he was the second best school administrator I met in thirty years? He was. That's the standard we've established. The waste in schools is staggering. People are hired and titles created for jobs nobody needs. There's waste in services contracted for; waste in supplies like books and milk; stupendous waste in precious time spent moving herds of children back and forth through corridors at the sound of a horn. In my experience, poor schools waste much more than rich schools, and rich schools waste more than you could believe.

The only public aspect of these places is that they function as a jobs project, although large numbers of these jobs are set aside as political patronage. Public schools can't understand how the average private school can make a profit on a per-seat cost less than half the "free" public charge; they can't understand how the average religious school makes do on even less. Homeschooling is the biggest puzzle of all. A principal once said to me, "Those people must be sick to spend so much time with children and not get paid for it!"

Consider the fantasy of teacher certification. Teachers are licensed and paid as though they are specialists, but they rarely are. For example, a science teacher is almost never actually a scientist — a man or woman who thinks about the secrets of nature as a private passion and pursues this interest on personal time. How many science classes in this country actually make any serious attempt to discover anything or to add to human knowledge? They are orderly ways of killing time, nothing more.

Kids are set to memorizing science vocabulary, repeating well-worn procedures certain to work, chanting formulas exactly as they have been indoctrinated to chant commercials from TV. The science teacher is a publicist for political truths set down in state-approved science textbooks.

Anyone who thinks school science is the inevitable precursor of real science is very innocent, indeed; of a piece, I think, with those poor, intelligent souls who, aware that television destroys the power to think by providing pre-seen sights, pre-thought thoughts, and unwholesome fantasies, still believe somehow that PBS television must be an exception to the rule.

If you would like to know how scientists are really made, pick up a wonderful book called *Discovering*, by Robert Scott Root-Bernstein. In it you'll learn from a prominent scientist himself that not one major scientific discovery of this century, including exotica like superconductivity, came from an academic laboratory, or a corporate or government laboratory, or a school laboratory. You could have guessed the last, but I surprised you with the others, didn't I? All came from garages, attics, and basements; all were managed with cheap, simple equipment and eccentric, personalized procedures of investigation. School is a perfect place to turn science into a religion, but it's the wrong place to learn science, for sure.

The specialists in English, math, social studies, and the rest of the rainbow of progressive subjects are only marginally more competent, if at all. If three million teachers were actually the specialists their licenses claim, they would be a major voice in national life and policymaking; if we are honest, we must wonder how it is possible for an army so large to be so silent, of such little consequence, in spite of the new hokum being retailed about "school-based management."

Don't misunderstand me. Teachers are frequently good people, intelligent people, talented people who work very hard. But regardless of how bright they are, how gracefully they "schoolteach," or how well they control children's behavior (which is, after all, what they are hired to do; if they can't do that, they are fired, but if they can, little else really matters), the net result of their efforts and our expense is surely very little or even nothing; indeed, often it leaves children worse off in terms of mental development and character formation than they were before being "taught." Schools that seem to be successful almost always are made to appear so by selective enrollment of self-motivated children.

The best way into the strange world of compulsory schooling is through books. I always knew real books and schoolbooks were different, but I didn't become conscious of the particulars until I got weary one day of New York City's brainless English curriculum and decided to teach Moby Dick to mainstream eighth-grade English classes. I discovered that the white whale is too big for the forty-five minute bell breaks of a junior high school. I couldn't make it "fit." But the editors of the school edition of Moby Dick had provided a package of prefabricated questions and nearly a hundred interpretations of their own. Every chapter began and ended with a barrage of these interventions. I came to see that the school edition wasn't a real book at all but a disguised indoctrination. The book had been rendered teacher-proof and student-proof.

This type of jigsaw fragmentation, designed to make the job site safe from its employees, is usually credited to Frederick Taylor's work of sinister genius, *Scientific Management*, written at the turn of this century. But that is wrong. The system was really devised before the American Revolution, in eighteenth-century Prussia, by Frederick the Great, and honed to perfection in early nineteenth-century Prussia after its humiliating defeat by Napoleon in 1806. A new system of schooling was the instrument out of which Prussian vengeance was shaped, a system that reduced human beings during their malleable years to reliable machine parts, human machinery dependent upon the state for its mission and purpose. When Blucher's Death's Head Hussars destroyed Napoleon at Waterloo, the value of Prussian schooling was confirmed.

By 1819, Prussian philosophy had given the world its first laboratory of compulsory schooling. That same year Mary Shelley wrote *Frankenstein*, the story of a German intellectual who fabricated a monster out of the parts of dead bodies; compulsory schooling was the monster she had in mind, emblemized in the lurching destruction caused by a homeless, synthetic creature seeking its maker, a creature with the infinite inner pain that ambiguous family brings.

In the nineteenth century, ties between Prussia and the United States were exceedingly close, a fact unknown these days because it became embarrassing to us during the World Wars and so was removed from history books. American scholarship during the nineteenth century was almost exclusively German at its highest levels, another fact conveniently absent from popular history. From 1814 to 1900, more than fifty thousand young men from prominent American families made the pilgrimage to Prussia and other parts of Germany to study under its new system of higher education based on research instead of "teaching." Ten thousand brought back Ph.D.s to a then-uncredentialed United States, preempting most of the available intellectual and technical work.

Prussian education was the national obsession among American political leaders, industrialists, clergy, and university people. In 1845, the Prussian emperor was even asked to adjudicate the boundary between Canada and the United States. Virtually every founding father of American compulsory schooling went to Prussia to study its clockwork schoolrooms firsthand. Horace Mann's *Seventh Report To The Boston School Committee of 1844* was substantially devoted to glowing praise of Prussian accomplishments and how they should become our own. Victor Cousin's book on Prussian schooling was the talk of our country about the same time. When, only a quarter-century later, Prussia crushed France in a brief war and performed the miracle of unifying Germany, it seemed clear that the way to unify our immigrant classes — which we so desperately sought to do — was through Prussian schooling.

By 1905, Prussian-trained Americans, or Americans like John Dewey who apprenticed at Prussian-trained hands, were in command of every one of our new institutions of scientific teacher training: Columbia Teacher's College, the University of Chicago, Johns Hopkins, the University of Wisconsin, Stanford. The domination of Prussian vision, and the general domination of German philosophy and pedagogy, was a *fait accompli* among the leadership of American schooling.

You should care about this for the compelling reason that German practices were used here to justify removal of intellectual material from the curriculum. It may explain why your own children cannot think. That was the Prussian way — to train only a leadership cadre to think.

Of all the men whose vision excited the architects of the new Prussianized American school machine, the most exciting were a German philosopher named Hegel and a German doctor named Wilhelm Wundt. In Wundt's laboratory the techniques of psychophysics (what today we might call "experimental psychology") were refined. Thanks to his work, it took only a little imagination to see an awesome new world emerging — for Wundt had demonstrated convincingly to his American students that people were only complex machines.

Man a machine! The implications were exhilarating, promising liberation from the ancient shackles of tradition, culture, morality, and religion. "Adjustment" became the watchword of schools and social welfare offices. G. Stanley Hall, one of Wundt's personal protegés (who as a professor at Johns Hopkins had inoculated his star pupil, John Dewey, with the German vines), now joined with Thorndike, his German-trained colleague at Columbia Teacher's College, to beat the drum for national standardized testing. Hall shrewdly sponsored and promoted an American tour for the Austrian doctor Sigmund Freud so that Freud might popularize his theory that parents and family were the cause of virtually all maladjustment — all the more reason to remove their little machines to the safety of schools.

In the minds of disciples of German educational thought, scientific education was primarily a way of forcing people to fit. With such a "technical" goal in mind, the future course of American schooling was determined, and with massive financial support from the foundations — especially those of the Rockefeller and Carnegie families — new scientific colleges to shape teachers were established. In Prussia these were aptly called "teacher seminaries," but here secular religionists were more discreet; a priesthood of trained professionals would guard the new school/church and write its canonical text into state law. Thus the Torah of twentieth-century compulsory schooling was in its Ark by 1895, one third of the way through the reign of William Torrey Harris as U.S. Commissioner of Education.

Teacher training in Prussia was founded on three premises, which the United States subsequently borrowed. The first of these is that the state is sovereign, the only true parent of children. Its corollary is that biological parents are the enemies of their offspring. When Germany's Froebel invented Kindergarten, it was not a garden for children he had in mind but a garden *of* children, in which state-appointed teachers were the gardeners of the children. Kindergarten is meant to protect children from their own mothers.

The second premise of Prussian schooling is that intellectual training is not the purpose of state schooling — obedience and subordination are. In fact, intellectual training will invariably subvert obedience unless it is rigidly controlled and doled out as a reward for obedience. If the will could be broken all else would follow. Keep in mind that will-breaking was the central logic of child-rearing among our own Puritan colonists, and you will see the natural affinity that exists between Prussian seeds and Puritan soil — from which agriculture our compulsory schooling law springs. The best-known device to break the will of the young, practiced for centuries among English and German upper classes, was the separation of parent and child at an early age. Here now was an institution backed by the power of the state to guarantee that separation. But it was not enough to compel obedience by intimidation. The child must be brought to love its synthetic parent. When George Orwell's protagonist in *1984* realizes that he loves Big Brother after betraying his lover to the state, we have a dramatic embodiment of the erotic destination of Prussian-type schooling.

The third premise of Prussian training is that the schoolroom and the workplace shall be dumbed down into simplified fragments that anyone, however dull, can memorize and operate. This solves the historical dilemma of leadership; a disobedient work force could be replaced quickly, without damage to production, if the workers required only habit, not mind, to function properly. This strategy paid off during the national strike of air traffic controllers a few years ago, when the entire force of these supposed "experts" was replaced overnight by management personnel and hastily trained fill-ins. There was no increase in accidents across the system! If anyone can do any particular job there's no reason to pay them very much except to guarantee employee loyalty and dependency — a form of love which bad parents often extort from their young in the same way.

In the training ground of the classroom, everything is reduced to bits under close management control. This allows progress to be quantified into precise rankings to track students throughout their careers — the great irony being that it's not intellectual growth that grades and reports really measure, but obedience to authority. That's why regular disclosures about the lack of correlation between standardized test scores and performance do not end the use of these surveillance mechanisms. What they actually measure is the tractability of the student, and this they do quite accurately. Is it of value to know who is docile and who may not be? You tell me.

Finally, if workers or students have little or no idea how their own part fits into the whole, if they are unable to make decisions, grow food, build a home or boat, or even entertain themselves, then political and economic stability will reign because only a carefully screened and seasoned leadership will know how things work. Uninitiated citizens will not even know what questions should be asked, let alone where the answers might be found. This is sophisticated pedagogy indeed, if far from what Mother and Father expect when they send Junior to school. This is what the religious Right is talking about when it claims that schooling is a secular religion. If you can think independently of pre-thought thoughts and received wisdom, you must certainly arrive at the same conclusion, whatever your private theology. Schooling is our official state religion; in no way is it a neutral vehicle for learning.

The sheer craziness of what we do to our children should have been sufficient cause to stop it once the lunacy was manifest in increased social pathology, but a crucial development forestalled corrective action: schooling became the biggest business of all. Suddenly there were jobs, titles, careers, prestige, and contracts to protect. As a country we've never had the luxury of a political or a religious or a cultural consensus. As a synthetic state, we've had only economic consensus; unity is achieved by making everyone want to get rich, or making them envy those who are.

Once a splendid economic machine like schooling was rolling, only a madman would try to stop it or to climb off its golden ascent. True, its jobs didn't seem to pay much (although its contractors did and do make fortunes), but upon closer inspection they paid more than most. And the security for the obedient was matchless because the institution provided the best insurance that a disturbing social mobility (characteristic of a frontier society) could finally be checked. Horace Mann, Henry Barnard, William Harris, Edward Thorndike, William James, John Dewey, Stanley Hall, Charles Judd, Ellwood Cubberly, James Russell — all the great schoolmen of American history — made endless promises to industrialists and old-line American families of prominence that if the new Prussian scheme were given support, prospects of a revolution here would vanish. (What a great irony that in a revolutionary nation the most effective motivator of leadership was the guarantee that another one could be prevented!)

Schools would be the insurance policy for a new industrial order which, as an unfortunate by-product of its operations, would destroy the American family, the small farmer, the landscape, the air, the water, the religious base of community life, the time-honored covenant that Americans could rise and fall by their own efforts. This industrial order would destroy democracy itself, and the promise held out to common men and women that if they were ever backed into a corner by their leaders, they might change things overnight at the ballot box.

I hope you can see now that this Prussian theory of workplaces and schools isn't just some historical oddity, but is necessary to explain customary textbook structure and classroom procedures, which fly in the face of how people actually learn. It explains the inordinate interest the foundations of Rockefeller and Carnegie took in shaping early compulsory schooling around a standardized factory model, and it sheds light on many mysterious aspects of modern American culture.

Compulsory schooling has been, from the beginning, a scheme of indoctrination into the new concept of mass man, an important part of which was the creation of a proletariat. According to Auguste Comte (surely the godfather of scientific schooling), you could create a useful proletariat class by breaking connections between children and their families, their communities, their God, and themselves. Remember William Harris's belief that self-alienation was the key to successful schooling? Of course it is. These connections have to be broken to create a dependable citizenry because, if left alive, the loyalties they foster are unpredictable and unmanageable. How can states operate that way?

Think of government schooling as a vast behavior clinic designed to create a harmless proletariat, the most important part of which is a professional proletariat of lawyers, doctors, engineers, managers, government people, and schoolteachers. This professional proletariat is held hostage by its addiction to luxury and security, and by its fear that the licensing monopoly might be changed by any change in governance. The main service it renders — advice — is contaminated by self-interest. We are all dying from it, the professional proletariat faster than anyone. It is their children who commit literal suicide with such regularity, not the children of the poor.

Printing questions at the end of chapters is a deliberate way of dumbing down a text to make it teacher-proof. We've done it so long that nobody examines the premises under the practice or sees the permanent reduction in mental sovereignty it causes. Just as science teachers were never supposed to be actual scientists, literature teachers weren't supposed to be original thinkers who brought original questions to the text.

In 1926, Bertrand Russell said casually that the United States was the first nation in human history to deliberately deny its children the tools of critical thinking; actually Prussia was first, we were second. The school edition of *Moby Dick* asked all the right questions, so I had to throw it away. Real books don't do that. They let readers actively participate with their own questions. Books that show you the best questions to ask aren't just stupid, they hurt the intellect under the guise of helping it, just as standardized tests do.

Well-schooled people, like schoolbooks, are very much alike. Propagandists have known for a century that school-educated people are easier to lead than ignorant people — as Dietrich Bonhoeffer confirmed in his studies of Nazism.

It's very useful for some people that our form of schooling tells children what to think about, how to think about it, and when to think about it. It's very useful to some groups that children are trained to be dependent on experts, to react to titles instead of judging the real men and women who hide behind the titles. It isn't very healthy for families and neighborhoods, cultures and religions. But then school was never about those things anyway; that's why we don't have them around anymore.

I think it would be fair to say that the overwhelming majority of people who make schools work today are unaware why they fail to give us successful human beings, no matter how much money is spent or how much good will is expended on reform efforts. This explains the inevitable temptation to find villains and to cast blame on bad teaching, bad parents, bad children, or penurious taxpayers.

The thought that school may be a brilliantly conceived social engine that works exactly as it was designed to work and produces exactly the human products it was designed to produce establishes a different relation to the usual demonologies. Seeing school as a triumph of human ingenuity, as a glorious success, forces us to consider whether we want this kind of success, and if not, to envision something of value in its place. And it forces us to challenge whether there is a "we," a national consensus sufficient to justify looking for one right way rather than dozens or even hundreds of right ways. I don't think there is.

Museums and institutes of useful knowledge travel a different road than schools. Consider the difference between librarians and schoolteachers. Librarians are custodians of real books and real readers; schoolteachers are custodians of schoolbooks and indentured readers. Somewhere in the difference is the Rosetta Stone that reveals how education is one thing, schooling another.

Begin with the setting and social arrangement of a library. The ones I've visited all over the country invariably are comfortable and quiet, places where you can read rather than just pretend to read. How important this silence is. Schools are never silent.

People of all ages work side by side in libraries, not just a pack of age-segregated kids. For some reason, libraries do not segregate by age, nor do they presume to segregate readers by questionable tests of reading ability. Just as the people who decoded the secrets of farming or of the forests and oceans were not segregated by age or test scores, the library seems to have intuited that common human judgment is adequate to most learning decisions.

The librarian doesn't tell me what to read, doesn't tell me the sequence of reading I have to follow, doesn't grade my reading. Librarians trust their customers. The librarian lets me ask my own questions and helps me when I need help, not when the library decides I need it. If I feel like reading in the same place all day long, that seems to be okay with the library. It doesn't tell me to stop reading at regular intervals by ringing a bell in my ear. The library keeps its nose out of my home, too. It doesn't send letters to my mother reporting on my library behavior; it doesn't make recommendations or issue orders on how I should use my time spent outside of the library.

The library doesn't have a tracking system. Everyone is mixed together there, and no private files exist detailing my past victories and defeats as a patron. If the books I want are available, I get them by requesting them — even if that deprives some more gifted reader, who comes a minute later. The library doesn't presume to determine which of us is more qualified to read that book; it doesn't play favorites. It is a very class-blind, talent-blind place, appropriately reflecting our historic political ideals in a way that puts schools to shame.

The public library isn't into public humiliation. It never posts ranked lists of good and bad readers for all to see. Presumably it considers good reading its own reward, not requiring additional accolades, and it has resisted the temptation to hold up good reading as a moral goad to bad readers. One of the strangest differences between libraries and schools, in New York City at least, is that you almost never see a kid behaving badly in a library or waving a gun there — even though bad kids have exactly the same access to libraries as good kids do. Bad kids seem to respect libraries, a curious phenomenon which may well be an unconscious response to the automatic respect libraries bestow blindly on everyone. Even people who don't like to read like libraries from time to time; in fact, they are such generally wonderful places I wonder why we haven't made them compulsory — and all alike, of course, too.

Here's another angle to consider: the library never makes predictions about my general future based on my past reading habits, nor does it hint that my days will be happier if I read Shakespeare rather than Barbara Cartland. The library tolerates eccentric reading habits because it realizes that free men and women are often very eccentric.

And finally, the library has real books, not schoolbooks. Its volumes are not written by collective pens or picked by politically correct screening committees. Real books conform only to the private curriculum of each writer, not to the invisible curriculum of some collective agenda. The one exception to this is children's books — but no sensible child ever reads those things, so the damage from them is minimal.

Real books are deeply subversive of collectivization. They are the best known way to escape herd behavior, because they are vehicles transporting the reader into deep caverns of absolute solitude where nobody else can visit. No two people ever read the same great book. Real books disgust the totalitarian mind because they generate uncontrollable mental growth — and it cannot be monitored.

Television has entered the classroom because it is a collective mechanism and, as such, much superior to textbooks; similarly, slides, audio tapes, group games, and so on meet the need to collectivize, which is a central purpose of mass schooling. This is the famous "socialization" that schools do so well. Schoolbooks, on the other hand, are paper tools that reinforce school routines of close-order drill, public mythology, endless surveillance, global ranking, and constant intimidation. That's what the questions at the end of chapters are designed to do, to bring you back to a reality in which you are subordinate. Nobody really expects you to answer those questions, not even the teacher; they work their harm solely by being there. That is their genius. Schoolbooks are a crowd-control device. Only the very innocent and well-schooled see any difference between good ones and bad ones; both kinds do the same work. In that respect they are much like television programming, the function of which, as a plug-in narcotic, is infinitely more powerful than any trivial differences between good programs and bad.

Real books educate, schoolbooks school, and thus libraries and library policies are a major clue to the reform of American schooling. When you take the free will and solitude out of education it becomes schooling. You can't have it both ways.

How Public Are
Our Public Schools?

My subject here is the type of school that calls itself "public," the familiar compulsory school of recent American history. The word "public" itself is an interesting term that doesn't enter the language until the beginning of the modern era, and which, for much of its early existence, was far from a flattering designation. Indeed the public was usually considered to be a dangerous creature by the folks who ran governments, a thing to be tricked, cajoled or intimidated — kept out of the way of its betters — for most of the early history of the word. Yet there was always another and brighter side to the idea, too, a feeling that there was such a thing as shared destiny among men and women and a common welfare to regard. Public parks and public libraries are two beautiful manifestations of this happier way of looking at fellow citizens in the abstract as brothers and sisters to care for.

So we have this dark side of the word "public" and this light side of the word "public" coexisting together, too easily confused. One conveys an attitude of beneficence toward abstract humanity, as do parks and libraries which offer their treasures without discrimination or excessive control; and the other conveys an attitude of dislike and mistrust. Where "public" describes an unmitigated, unmistakable benefit, one commonly acknowledged to be a good thing, there we always find choice: an individual may take the benefit or leave it according to a private schedule or private taste. But where the word "public" covers an enterprise that most people would not choose, would not buy in a free market, there we always find forms of compulsion to make people swallow by force what they would not take willingly. The compulsion may be subtle in the form of constant drumbeating propaganda for orthodoxy, it may be accomplished through ridicule or praise, the familiar carrots and sticks of scientific marketing, or it may be open and flagrant as when taxing power is used to force citizens to buy what the police power of the state then forces them to consume.

So the two uses of "public" are a far cry from each other. One speaks to individual preferences and celebrates human difference as in the case of libraries and parks, and one speaks to a faith in uniformity and conformity as a way of controlling the public "for its own good." There are really no points of correspondence between the two notions at all, yet it isn't hard to see that an institution designed to control people might well find it useful to advertise that its motives are public in the popular sense, and its own people over time might even come to believe that.

Few public schools in the United States are truly public in the common sense of that term because to qualify for such a position a school has to illustrate by its procedures a respect for the public and its individual members. Recent attempts to offer parents and students fundamental choices in schooling have been regularly rebuffed by defenders of the government monopoly school with the contention that parents are unfit to make such decisions, that chaos would follow, that the public lacks genuine motivation to help its children or sufficient knowledge or skill, that we would return to a dark age if the school establishment was not guaranteed exclusive use of public taxes and exclusive use of authority to compel its clientele to assemble. You may decide for yourself which of the two attitudes toward the public is demonstrated by such argument.

If public schools were truly public, we would find in their internal workings evidence they tended to realize public will, both the larger national dreams and the smaller local ones of regions, communities, neighborhoods, and families. If a classless society is the national dream, as for most of our history it has seemed to be in the United States, then schools would be classless in honor of this yearning, as one-room school houses were. If democracy was deemed the national form of government by popular will, we could reasonably expect schools to offer daily practice in democracy. If independence and self-sufficiency was an important national goal, then in farm, forest, and waterfront communities we would look to public schools to assume a heavy responsibility for the stewardship of the natural world, and in large cities, public schools would focus the attention of the young on the precarious life-support systems that make urban life possible — and recruit their assistance in preserving these.

Yet virtually nowhere in these places do we find anything but rigid practices which discourage the democratic spirit (and which certainly have played a major part in discouraging seventy-five percent of our electorate from voting), and virtually nowhere do we find public schools offering a course of study responsive to the public will or taking part in any convincing effort for the common good. Public schools, by draining the enthusiasm and energy of children from common public concerns, and by draining vast resources from public taxes, behave more like a parasite on the public bloodstream than a resource like parks and libraries.

Over three decades of work in schools I came to realize that the concrete institution of public school is a terrible way to realize the abstract public ideal of education for all. Public schools and public education are not the same thing. We are bewildered into silence by semantic looseness allowing a lobby for government schooling to claim it has a monopoly on public education. Schooling and education are not the same thing.

Schools are a business having very little to do with education. Until we recognize the differences, we must concede the field to the very government agencies, school suppliers, colleges, unions, and other special interests that created the mess we are in. It is important also to realize that these interests flourish particularly well in a climate of alarm, decay, and collapse. Surely it is an immense irony that if our children were doing well, the people who make a living from their trouble would not be.

Around the year 1850 all the free-form, casual schooling that made our nation of farmers far and away the best-educated the world had ever seen was done away with in a series of strokes of the legislative pen. It was killed by state decree. Schools would henceforth be compulsory. That strange notion had been a dream of social engineers for thousands of years, but no place had it ever been accepted. But in the early nineteenth century, in the region of Germany known as Prussia, it was. That's where Horace Mann got the model he needed, from Prussia. Our own Puritans passed several compulsion laws, but unable to enforce them allowed them to wither. Suddenly in the panic and confusion of Catholic immigration a law was rammed home by the Know-Nothing legislature of

Massachusetts. No popular vote was ever held on this decision; if one had been it would have been crushingly defeated. No public debates were held about the inception of monopoly schooling except among elites in a few local jurisdictions. This wildly radical act was simply "done."

In what real sense was this new institution "public" when it was opposed everywhere? In what sense was it decent in a democracy? In what sense is anything accomplished by police compulsion or indifference to public will "public"? I hope you agree that is a legitimate question that strikes to the root of something important which might explain the failure of our government schools.

Certainly such an institutional creature is public in a very peculiar sense if we are honest about it. In about the same way, I think, that the poisoned air of Los Angeles is public air because all Angelenos are compelled to breathe it — even though only a few are responsible for making it. Some people will say schools are public because they are free, but that assertion has a certain madness to it when we confront the reality these free public seats cost well over twice as much as "private" school seats or church school seats; and about twelve times as much as a homeschool seat. Perhaps, then, our public schools can be called "public" because they mix all the public together for instruction. But that comforting notion dissolves under a visit to a public school anywhere in urban or suburban America. It dissolves everywhere under the omnipresent class system which divides children into classes and the "tracking" system which divides children into castes, and it dissolves under examination of private and church schools which prove upon inspection to be better integrated than their so-called public counterparts if a Brookings Institute report can be trusted.

What on earth is going on? Twenty-nine children were shot in New York City public schools from January 1 to the end of March 1992 when I stopped counting — and not a single one in private or parochial schools, nor in any homeschools either. Surely the right to die in school isn't what makes them public. If schools were public in any defensible meaning of that term then the public would be satisfied with them most of the time; over long periods we should be able to trace clear public agreement that what they were doing made sense, was pleasing, was the right thing to do. Conversely, if people are dissatisfied with schools decade after decade, then only in "Newspeak," Orwell's language of tyranny, could there be anything public in such schools.

If you are willing to concede that people want and need different things, and further to concede that individuals must almost always be the judges of what is best for their development if we are to have a free society, then it will quickly be seen that all varieties of schooling that are voluntary and not unfairly exclusionary are public schools. If the exclusive government seizure of all educational tax monies was stopped and a fair and equitable distribution begun, then almost all schools, of any type, would be "free," too. We have things backwards. Only schools that command attendance and command their parent clientele to obey cannot be called public schools; calling compulsory monopoly institutions "public," when they are the only variety which is not, is a feat of doublespeak equal to saying that war is peace, up is down, black is white.

The idea that a government can enforce thought-control on its masses while at the same time doing something for the common good was an exhausted notion from the very beginning. No one can dispute that it is possible to control the way people think, to control what they think about, and even the conclusions they reach. You need only look at how governments manage war-making or television manages political images to see how that is done. And on the other hand it is also indisputable that astonishing services can be provided to the intellect, character, and spirit of a young human being through the intervention of older heads. But it is impossible to do both those things at once; they are in permanent dialectical opposition, polar opposites. Both goals, central control and individual power, set irresistible forces in motion which are hostile to one another, hence they cannot coexist in the same human being without psychological disturbance occurring.

Controlling the minds of others until they reflexively respond as you want them to is what schooling is about. It arises from a belief, usually unexamined, that people are machines — in theological terms, predestined. But education is a much different animal. It is alive, singular, different for every single human being. Education arises from a belief that in each of us a unique blueprint waiting to unfold lies hidden. This is an idea from the world of nature, just as schooling is an idea from the world of machines; unlike the machine world education revels in risk-taking, adventure, variety, surprise, and challenge.

"First, know thyself." That directive is the *sine qua non* of all educational systems. That is an unavoidable beginning and it takes years of intense private struggle to accomplish. Kids need significant private time and significant common responsibility to know themselves; if the procedure is too long delayed hideous lifelong difficulties ensue. Indeed, interfering with the appointments young people must keep in order to know themselves has long been understood as the way to create a proletariat class, a mass of cheap labor without mind or loyalty, direction or purpose — a class with slavish habits able to be led or intimidated as circumstances warrant.

Our system of monopoly compulsory schooling guarantees to ruin the prospects of knowing oneself for a very long time. The tests one must pass to know himself are tests of action and quiet reflection, tests passed only by meeting painful challenges; paper and pencil tests stupefy the character and corrupt the mind. They are good tools from which to fashion a servant class but they ruin independent spirits in embryo. Education in some vital sense is all wrapped up in the notion of free will; however much we may wish to shy away from the theological controversies of history, when we set out to school a nation it is, inevitably, a religion we are seeking to impose, even if we don't call it that. We are aiming to control the public myths and without such control, as Plato saw, governors have no reliable way to engineer the governed.

A little while ago I said that it was known from the beginning that government monopoly schools would not work, if by "work," we mean being broadly useful. I can begin to prove that to you if you'll listen to the voices from history for a while. I don't have time to make a comprehensive case, but even in a short presentation of the public record on schooling I think you'll be surprised enough to wonder why you haven't heard these things before.

Remember that for the first 200 years of our history schooling was cheap, competitive, and voluntary — and if de Tocqueville and our sensational accomplishments are to be believed, quite successful. School was everywhere considered a good thing, but absolutely nowhere considered a very essential thing because it was common knowledge then that learning to read, write, and do arithmetic are easy things to learn, even on one's own and even by the poor, with a little work. And they are not terribly difficult to become proficient at, either. People, it was widely understood, could grow up bright, alert, decent, competent, and prosperous — even scholarly and profound — without much schooling at all. The idea of people sitting in a chair year-round would have been thought insane.

Have you ever wondered what the best people thought as they watched the new institution of compulsory schooling unfold in the last half of the nineteenth century, and what they thought as they watched its first phalanx of graduates take their place in the world? Herbert Spencer, the great British philosopher and publicist of Darwinism, wrote a remarkable book entitled *Education* in the early 1860s in which he pronounced government schooling a preposterous endeavor doomed to failure. He said that this would happen because it deprived children of raw experience and responsibility precisely at the moment their natural development demanded it, and that this experience and responsibility could not be made up for later. In 1867 a prominent American physician, Vincent Youmans, argued before the London College of Preceptors that the new system was the creation of lunatics. "It produces mental perversion and absolute stupidity," he said. "It produces bodily disease. It produces these things by measures which operate to the prejudice of the growing brain. It is not to be doubted that dullness, indocility, and viciousness" are taught by the lessons of school. The author of the famous book *Parkman's Journal* spoke out in 1880, saying "schools have not borne fruit on which we have cause to congratulate ourselves."

From 1860 to 1880 there is no evidence in the historical record that a Golden Age of government monopoly schooling existed. If there was ever one it had to occur after those years.

In 1885 the president of Columbia University spoke as follows: "The results attained under our present system of instruction are neither very flattering nor very encouraging." In 1895 the president of Harvard said this: "Ordinary schooling, by confining children to books and withdrawing their attention from visible objects, renders the senses useless. It produces dumbness. A young man whose intellectual powers are worth cultivating cannot be willing to cultivate them by pursuing the phantoms the schools insist upon."

When those words were spoken, monopoly schooling was approaching its fiftieth year as a new institution, but still no signs of a Golden Age were about. School was producing "dumbness" in the quaint language of the time.

Jumping ahead thirty-five years to 1930 we find the subject of the high-powered annual Inglis Lecture at Harvard to be public schooling. Its central thesis was this: "We have absolutely nothing to show for our colossal investment in common schooling after eighty years of trying." Absolutely nothing. As far as Cambridge was concerned the Golden Age of government schooling, then, was a pipe dream. The Golden Age, if it exists, must lie beyond 1930, it certainly can't be before that date.

On the lip of our own age, John Gardner's "Annual Report to the Carnegie Corporation," in 1960, said this: "The emphasis upon formal schooling has been exaggerated beyond all reason ... the failure to see constructive alternatives is leading us into deeper and deeper absurdities. Too many young people gain nothing except the conviction they are misfits."

It seems if we are to find a Golden Age to justify a government monopoly on the way young people think, to justify a government monopoly on the way they grow up, to justify the government monopoly on what they are told the purpose of existence is, then we must search for that justification in the years from 1960 to 1992. Unless we find a Golden Age there, after 142 years of trying, isn't it time to say, "Enough!"?

Well, there is a Golden Age there, but not the kind the public might expect as its due. In inflation adjusted dollars we now spend four times more in 1992 than we did in 1930; it has been a Golden Age without parallel for schoolmen and school suppliers and local politicians. A golden river overflowing its banks. Millions of people make an excellent living on the backs of 40 million young lives forced into government containers, tens of thousands of suppliers grow quite rich this way, independent of what happens to the children. It is the best of businesses: exclusive, unfailingly profitable, undemanding, and guaranteed year after year by the power of the state. Where in the America of the Bill of Rights and the Revolution is such an institution part of the covenant?

Schools at present are the occupation of our children. Children have become pensioners of the government at an early age. They have make-work jobs, not really jobs at all — there is nothing asked of children in government schools that is real, there is nothing important to do there. Only one performance act is demanded by the state just as it is demanded with all other types of made-up government work: the children must attend. They must be present through the school day as they are passed from stranger to stranger to the sound of horns in this eerie form of growing up they have been assigned.

Children are condemned to hours of desperation in schools, pretending to do work that doesn't exist. School is a liar's world, it cannot deliver on its promises; at the end of each day children are full of aggression which they take out on their families. School children are sad and desperate people, they recognize they are dying but don't understand how the execution is being managed. They are the developmental stages of a proletariat in the making, without heart, without initiative, without knowledge of their own families or histories and without any abiding loyalties. Their spirits are broken on a government dole which in a short time becomes addictive. Even when they are offered real work to do, most drift back to the secure meaninglessness of busy work. Anyone who has ever tried to lead public school students into generating lines of meaning in their own lives will have felt the hostility with which broken children fight to be left alone. "Just tell me what to do," they say through gritted teeth.

If the school day and the school year are enlarged to include dawn to dusk confinement as some experts are proposing, students will become workers forbidden to leave their offices. Schools already consume most of the people they hold, teachers included; in the new world order nothing at all is to be left unchained, apparently. The specious argument that summer vacation should be curtailed or eliminated because children no longer have to farm leaves out of its calculations that children have to run and play freely in the Sun, which like themselves is young once only, if they are to grow up with free will, to be actors instead of agents. Where you stand on this issue has nothing to do with reading and arithmetic, but much to do with what you find the meaning of life to be — it is, at bottom, a religious question.

School curricula are like bad economies. Like our own cash economy has become, schools don't deal in basic industries, instead they try by magic tricks and scary illusions to hold down rebellion. Because educated people are not attracted to schooling, these places must deal in the light stuff; that's why even the brightest kids can't read well anymore. Only one person in ten reads more than one book a year after they graduate from our schools according to the American Librarian's Association. In the inflationary economy of mass schooling, with its crazy "A"s and crazier gold stars, handshakes, and trophies — none of which are tied to anything real — sensible people lose their grip and become unable to function sensibly in their own best interests. In a madhouse you're happy just to make it to the end of the day. Real learning is always its own reward and praise is as useless to it as punishment.

Once the inflation of dishonesty is perceived, as it is by almost all school kids past third grade, the phantom curriculum can only be imposed by a cacophony of bells and horns and shouted orders, by tests and busyness, confusion and threats. With inflation of the school variety you can't even surrender; the state demands that you acknowledge school time to be valuable or you are liable to severe sanctions. If schools didn't insist on ritual loyalties and compulsory attendance everyone would leave except the teachers who are being paid. Is there anyone out there who doesn't understand this? Schools are always the arena of crisis because they prevent children from preparing for the future and prevent families from finding sanctuary and significance with each other. Schools have forced children out of the true economy of meanings, where nobody has to be urged to grow up, and into an empty fantasy economy of gold stars and grades and other worthless pay-offs. To survive as schoolpeople we have to do things that are unethical. We keep kids longer and longer out of the world of human beings and nature. We corruptly make jobs depend on school time and course work even when we are absolutely certain they have no demonstrable connection with such things.

You've just heard me speak in a somewhat abstract way about the psychopathology of government schooling and of some processes that produce the strange children who populate our world. I want you to begin to think about depriving the government of its taxes which pay for schools and to think, too, about restoring free will choice to every taxpayer and family, rich and poor. I want you to help restore the kind of market in schooling we had for the first 200 years of our history before a fear of Catholic immigration put your children's lives into the hands of social engineers.

Without free will choices in matters as important as how your children will be taught to think, you are reduced to the status of machines, to be switched on and off and programmed in your functions by the shadowy elite which has always sought to control what it calls "the public."

For my own part, as a former New York State Teacher of the Year and a former New York City Teacher of the Year, I feel ashamed and angry that I acted as an agent of government monopoly schooling for so many years; it is a thing that hurts almost every life it touches. I feel ashamed as a citizen that we have retreated so far from the covenant of the Bill of Rights we agreed to just three lifetimes ago. And I feel ashamed that so many of us cannot imagine a better way to do things than locking children up all day in cells instead of letting them grow up knowing their families, mingling with the world, assuming real obligations, striving to be independent and self-reliant and free.

I've spoken to you today about the effects of conceding the government plan to be a "public" plan when it is nothing of the sort. But I spoke as a longtime schoolteacher bearing witness to his own observations and his own part in the tragedy. Now I want you to hear someone else speak. During the year I was New York State Teacher of the Year, 1800 people wrote letters to me from every state in the Union and from seven foreign countries. The most amazing thing about these letters is that they are all really about the same thing — all are public outcries against being compelled to be a character in someone else's story. Listen as hard as you can to these voices, they all belong to real people with real names from real places.

- Sacramento: I can remember being six years old and watching the clock in school thinking, "Oh, no, God, there can't be twelve more years of this."

- Toronto: My wife quit her job because we fear losing contact with our children as they enter a school system we cannot understand and are unable to change. Little is different since the days I was asked to sit in straight rows and memorize an irrelevant curriculum.

• Tacoma: My passion is that my daughter be allowed to grow up completely who she is and right now she is a happy, enthusiastic, self-taught child of eight-and-a-half. She taught herself to read at four, reads everything. School to me has always felt incorrect and sick at the core.

• Reno: My wife and I came to the end of the rope with public schools four years ago. I was tired of seeing my once happy child constantly in tears.

• Santa Barbara: I just took my eight-year-old daughter from school. Bit by bit she was becoming silent and fearful. From her anxiety to reach the school bus on time to the times she was visibly shaken from criticism of her homework, day by day she was changing before my eyes for the worse. But the absolute end was the destructive effect the culture of school children's values had on her behavior. It was *Lord of the Flies* come to life. Now she laughs again. I have my laughing girl back.

• Pittsburgh: School started to destroy my family by dividing us from each other. It created separatism among the kids, among the classes, among the ages, among the races, among parents and children. After I took my second grader from school she began to blossom. Now she loves her time; the time is the gift.

• Memphis: I defined myself as a child by my accomplishments at school just as I had been taught to. I was a National Merit

Scholar and a Presidential Scholar, too, but I couldn't even make it through two years of college because my own authoritarian upbringing had left me completely unprepared to make my own decisions.

- Kansas City: Mr. Gatto, you are describing my daughter when you name the pathologies our children acquire as a result of their schooling. And you are describing me, which pains me almost unbearably to recognize and admit.

- Haverhill, MA: I have no certificates of great accomplishment, no titles, not a diploma except a high school one, no degrees except when I have a fever, yet I do have experience gained while raising three daughters. I'd like to paint a picture for you: I had to take my daughter out of kindergarten, my youngest one, after just five weeks. This happy, self-regulating child I was raising showed great signs of stress in that short of a time. I remembered the rebellion of my two angry teenagers suddenly, put two and two together, and took the youngest from school. And so the last child I raised was raised as a free child. And there have been no signs of anger or rebellion since. That was seventeen years ago.

School presents us with a liar's world. On no level, not even first grade, do school personnel tell the truth about what they are doing. And to be fair, most of them don't know what the truth is; schooling is a job to be done as well as possible, but not to be questioned, just to be done. A thousand times I heard the advice during my pubic school years, "Don't rock the boat," but the boat is sinking from the dead weight of its dishonesty. Perhaps rocking it might spill out the cargo that's sinking it.

The philosophical base of compulsory schooling lies in disbelief that this is a moral universe and in a philosophy that we inhabit a dog-eat-dog world where material creatures compete for limited resources and need to be held in check. School's theoreticians do not believe in free will, holding instead that people are mechanisms, and that disaster would follow the release of central controls over children. From this base of ideas flows automatically certain structures of schooling known to be harmful. If you believe in free will and a moral universe, then the schooling you design will attempt to promote self-reliance, compassion, and free choice. If you believe that families are the basic institution of human life, then the schooling you design will have the intention to strengthen bonds of family. But if you believe that human beings are imperfect machines, wound up like bad clocks, then school becomes a field in which to implant habits, to install controls over group behavior, to form synthetic family associations in the hope of superseding real families. School becomes a place to teach everyone they cannot trust themselves or anybody else except the voice of authority.

Twentieth-century American government schools are compulsory behavior clinics with little interest in scholarship, as their own internal workings betray. They are the result of an ancient belief among mobile aristocracies, like our own Puritan classes, that the mass of humanity cannot be trusted, and is, indeed, dangerous. Our Puritan elites, like the Vikings they initially derived from, were nearly homeless in the grandest meaning of that term.

Always obsessed with controlling strangers they encountered on their wanderings, with killing Indians and enslaving Africans, with driving out the Spanish and the French, with hanging Quakers and hunting witches, this grand ungodly tormented people developed a religion which taught fear, suspicion, and distrust, which taught the damned could not be regenerated, but could only be confined, and kept under surveillance.

It is no accident our national school system took root in Puritan soil; schools such as we have could not have come from anywhere else. From a foundation of mistrust built in kindergarten, a foundation whose central tenet is that children do not learn but have to be taught, that children must be tricked into accepting responsibility by motivating them with worthless prizes, worthless praise, and plenty of good old-fashioned humiliation, from such a wellhead many hideous things crawl out naturally. From a foundation of mistrust, a technology of security and behavior-modification grows, a belief that young people must be shaped by the state, not by their own families, cultures, and communities.

So finally we arrive at the very schools we have, where parents are deprived by many clever means of significant influence over their own children, where a horde of synthetic family networks beckon to the lost children we have created with our synthetic tools of abstract intellect. From this world view of suspicion and envy we arrive at an economy where an estimated twenty-two percent of all our jobs are some form or another of surveillance work — surveillance, admonition, ranking, and punishment work, if the sequence be drawn out. When we begin to think of school reform we are feeling our way through an unmapped land because so many of us are the orphans and homeless children of mass schooling ourselves.

It is time to change all this. We need competition and choices in the forms children are offered to grow up by. We need this to restore sanity to our own lives as well as to the lives of children. One-right-way schooling in a compulsion monopoly system must be ended. There is no way to repair the present system, and if there were, who in his right mind would want to?

Nine Assumptions
and Twenty-One Facts

I'll start off bluntly by giving you some data I'd be shocked if you already know. A few simple facts, all verifiable, which by their existence call into question the whole shaky edifice of American schooling from kindergarten through college and its questionable connection with the job market. The implications of this data are quite radical so I'm going to take pains to ground it in the most conservative society on earth, the mountain world of Switzerland. You all remember Switzerland: that's where people put their money when they really want it to be really safe.

The Swiss just like us believe that education is the key to their national success, but that's where our similarity ends. In 1990 about sixty percent of American secondary school graduates enrolled in college, but only twenty-two percent did in Switzerland; in America almost one hundred percent of our kids go to high school or private equivalents, but only a little over a fifth of the Swiss kids do. And yet the Swiss per capita income is the highest of any nation in the world and the Swiss keep insisting that virtually everyone in their country is highly educated!

What on earth could be going on? Remember it's a sophisticated economy which produces the highest per-capita paycheck in the world we're talking about, high for the lightly-schooled as well as for the heavily schooled, higher than Japan's, Germany's or our own. No one goes to high school in Switzerland who doesn't also want to go to college; three-quarters of the young people enter apprenticeships before high school. It seems the Swiss don't make the mistake that schooling and education are synonyms.

If you are thinking silently at this point that apprenticeships as a substitute for classroom confinement isn't a very shocking idea and it has the drawback of locking kids away from later choice of white collar work, think again. I wasn't only talking about blue-collar apprenticeships — although the Swiss have those, too — but white-collar apprenticeships in abundance. Many of the top management of insurance companies, manufacturing companies, banks, etc., never saw the inside of a high school, let alone a college.

Shocking is the word for it, isn't it? I mean here you are putting away your loot in a Swiss bank because it's safe over there and not so safe here, and now I've told you the bank president may only have a sixth grade schooling. Just like Shakespeare did.

As long as we're playing "Did You Know?", did you know that in Sweden, a country legendary for its quality of life and a nation which beats American school performance in every academic category, a kid isn't allowed to start school before the age of seven? The hardheaded Swedes don't want to pay for the social pathologies attendant on taking a child away from his home and mother and dumping him into a pen with strangers. Can you remember the last time you worried about a Swedish Volvo breaking down prematurely or a Swedish jet engine failing in the air? Did you know that the entire Swedish school sequence is only nine years long, a net twenty-five percent time and tax savings over our own twelve-year sequence?

Exactly in whose best interest do you think it is that the *New York Times*, or every other element of journalism, for that matter, doesn't make information like this readily accessible? How can you think clearly about our own predicament if you don't have it?

Did you know that Hong Kong, a country with a population the size of Norway's, beats Japan in every scientific and mathematical category in which the two countries compete? Did you know that Hong Kong has a school year ten and one half weeks shorter than Japan's? How on earth do they manage that if longer school years translate into higher performance? Why haven't you heard about Hong Kong, do you suppose? You've heard enough about Japan, I'm sure.

But I'll bet you haven't heard this about Japan. I'll bet you haven't heard that in Japan a recess is held after every class period.

Or did you know that in Flemish Belgium, with the shortest school year in the developed world, that the kids regularly finish in the top three nations in the world in academic competition? Is it the water in Belgium or what? Because it can't be the passionate commitment to government schooling, which they don't seem to possess.

Did you know that three British Prime Ministers in this century including the current one didn't bother to go to college? I hope I've made the point. If you trust journalism or the professional educational establishment to provide you with data you need to think for yourself in the increasingly fantastic world of American schooling, you are certainly the kind of citizen who would trade his cow for a handful of colored beans.

Shortly into the twentieth century American schooling decided to move away from intellectual development or skills training as the main justification for its existence and to enter the eerie world of social engineering, a world where "socializing" and "psychologizing" the classroom preempted attention and rewards. Professionalization of the administrative/teaching staff was an important preliminary mechanism to this end, serving as a sieve to remove troublesome interlopers and providing lucrative ladders to reward allies and camp followers.

Nonintellectual, non-skill schooling was supported by a strange and motley collection of fellow travelers: from unions, yes, but also from the ranks of legendary businessmen like Carnegie and Rockefeller, Ford and Astor. There were genuine ideologues like John Dewey, yes, but many academic opportunists as well like Nicholas Murray Butler of Columbia. Prominent colleges like Johns Hopkins and the University of Chicago took a large hand in the deconstruction of American academic schooling as well as a powerful core of private foundations and think tanks. Whether they did this out of conviction, for the advantage of private interests, or any hybrid of these reasons and more I'll leave for the moment to others for debate. What is certain is that the outcomes aimed for had little to do with why parents thought children were ordered into schools.

In those early years of the twentieth century a radical shift was well under way, transforming a society of farmers and craftspeople, fishermen, and small entrepreneurs into the disciplined work force of a corporate state, one in which *all* the work was being sucked into colossal governments, colossal institutions and colossal business enterprises — a society whose driving logic was comfort, security, predictability and consensus rather than independence, originality, risk-taking and uncompromising principle. In the gospels of social engineering, this transformation was leading to a future utopia of welfare capitalism. With the problem of "production" solved, the attention of professional intellectuals and powerful men of wealth turned to controlling distribution so that a "rational" society, defined as a stable state without internal or external conflicts, could be managed for nations, regions, and eventually the entire planet. In such a system, if you behave, you get a share of the divvy and if you don't, your share is correspondingly reduced.

Keep in mind that a small farmer, a carpenter, a fisherman, or seamstress never gave undue attention to being well-behaved and you will begin to see how a centralized economy and centralized schooling box human behavior into a much narrower container than what it normally would occupy and you will begin to see why intellectual development, for all its theoretical desirability, can never really be a serious goal for a society seeking comfort, security, predictability and consensus. Indeed, such a fate must be actively avoided.

Anyway, once this design was in place — and it was firmly in place by 1917 — all that remained to reach the target was a continual series of experiments on public schoolchildren, some modest in scope, many breathtakingly radical like "IQ tests" or "kindergartens." Each of these thrusts has a real behavioral purpose which is part of the larger utopia envisioned, yet each is capable of being rhetorically defended as the particular redress of some current "problem."

But the biggest obstacle to a planned society is parents. Parents have their own plans for their own kids. Most often they love their kids, so their motivations are self-reinforcing, unlike those of schoolpeople who do it for a paycheck. Unless held in check, even a few unhappy parents can disrupt the conduct of an educational experiment.

The second biggest obstacle to a planned society are religious sects, each of which maintains that God has a plan for all human beings, including children. And the third biggest obstacle is local values and ethnic cultures which also provide serious maps for growing up.

Each of these three is an external force bidding for the loyalty of children against the directions of the political state which owns the schools. One final obstacle — and a colossal one — is the individual nature of each particular child. John Locke pulled a whopper when he maintained that children are blank slates waiting to be written upon. He should have asked a few mothers about that. The fact is that if you watch children closely in controlled conditions as I did for thirty years as a schoolteacher, you can hardly fail to conclude that each kid has a private destiny he or she is pulling toward wordlessly, a destiny frequently put out of reach by schoolteachers, school executives, or project officers from the Ford Foundation.

In a planned society individuality, cultural identity, and a relationship with God or a close-knit family are all elements which must be suppressed if they cannot be totally extinguished. The United States has been going down this road, with hesitations, at least since the end of the first world war. To accomplish such a complex transformation of nature into mechanism the general public must be led to agree to certain apparently sensible assumptions. Such as the assumption, for instance, that a college degree is necessary for a high-status career — even though Swiss corporations and the British government are often run by managers without college training.

The security of the school institution depends on many such assumptions, some which by adroit concealments worthy of a card sharp seem to link schooling and future responsibility, and some which serve to exalt the political state, diminish essential human institutions like the family, or define human nature as mean, violent, and brutish. I'd like to pass nine specimens drawn from these latter categories of assumption in front of your minds to allow each of you to gauge which ones you personally accept, and to what degree.

Nine Assumptions of Schooling

1. Social cohesion is not possible through other means than compulsory schooling; school is the main defense against social chaos.

2. Children cannot learn to tolerate each other unless first socialized by mentors.

3. The only safe mentors of children are certified experts with state-licensed conditioning; children must be protected from the uncertified.

4. Compelling children to violate family, cultural, and religious norms does not interfere with the development of their intellects or characters.

5. Children must be disabused of the notion that Mother and Father are sovereign in morality or intelligence.

6. Families should be encouraged to expend concern on the

general education of everyone, but discouraged from being unduly concerned with their own children's education.

7. The state has predominant responsibility for training, morals, and beliefs. Children who escape state scrutiny will become immoral.

8. Children from families with different beliefs, backgrounds and styles must be forced together even if those beliefs contradict one another.

9. Compulsion in the name of liberty is a valid use of state power.

These assumptions and a few others associated with them lead directly to the shape, style, and exercise of school politics. And these primary assumptions generate secondary assumptions which fuel the largely phony school debate played out in American journalism, a debate where the most important questions like "What is the end that justifies these means?" are never asked.

I once had dinner in Washington at the same table as Fred Hechinger, Education Editor of the *New York Times*. When I raised the possibility that the *Times* framed its coverage to omit inconvenient aspects of school questions (such as challenging the presumed connection between quantity of money spent and quality of education) Mr. Hechinger became angry and dismissed my contention; almost the same thing happened on a different occasion, also in Washington, when I had dinner at the Council for Basic Education at the same table with Albert Shanker of the American Federation of Teachers. With that history of failure in opening a dialogue with some of the powers and principalities of institutional education (and I could add Lamar Alexander, Bill Bennett, Joe

Fernandez, Diane Ravitch, Checker Finn and many other luminaries who seemed to hear me with impatience) I've been driven to trying to catch the ear of the general public in meeting the assumptions schools rely upon with contradictory facts open to formal verification, or the informal variety grounded in common sense. What follows are twenty-one of these disturbing contradictions raised for your contemplation:

Twenty-One Facts About Schooling

1. There is no relationship between the amount of money spent on schooling and "good" results as measured by parents of any culture. This seems to be because education is not a commodity to be purchased but an enlargement of insight, power, understanding, and self-control almost completely outside the cash economy. Education is almost overwhelmingly an internally generated effort. The five American states which usually spend least per capita on schooling are the five which usually have the best test results (although Iowa which is about thirtieth in spending sometimes creeps into the honored circle).

2. There is no compelling evidence to show a positive relationship between length of schooling and accomplishment. Many countries with short school years outperform those with long ones by a wide margin.

3. Most relationships between test scores and job performance are illegitimate, arranged in advance by only allowing those testing well access to the work. Would you hire a newspaper reporter because he had "A"s in English? Have you ever asked your surgeon

what grade he got in meat-cutting? George F. Kennan, intellectual darling of the Washington elite some while ago and the author of our "containment" policy against the Soviet Union often found his math and science grades in secondary school below sixty, and at Princeton he had many flunks, "D"s and "C"s. "Sometimes," he said, "it is the unadjusted student struggling to forge his own standards who develops within himself the thoughtfulness to comprehend." Dean Acheson, Harry Truman's Secretary of State, graduated from Groton with a sixty-eight average. The headmaster wrote his mother, "He is ... by no means a pleasant boy to teach." Einstein, we all know, was considered a high grade moron, as were Thomas Edison and Benjamin Franklin. Is there anybody out there who really believes that grades and test scores are the mark of the man?

4. Training done on the job is invariably cheaper, quicker, and of much higher quality than training done in a school setting. If you wonder why that should be, you want to start, I think, by understanding that training and education are two different things, one largely residing in the development of good habits, the other in the development of vision and understanding, judgment and the like. Education is self-training; it calls into its calculations mountains of personal data and experience which are simply unobtainable by any schoolteacher or higher pedagogue. That simple fact is why all the many beautifully precise rules on how to think produce such poor results.

5. In spite of relentless propaganda to the contrary, the American economy is tending strongly to require less knowledge and less intellectual ability of its employees, not more. Scientists and mathematicians currently exist in numbers far exceeding any global demand for them or any national demand, and that condition

should grow much worse over the next decade, thanks to the hype of pedagogues and politicians. Schools can be restructured to teach children to develop intellect, resourcefulness and independence, but that would lead, in short order, to structural changes in the economy so profound it is not likely to be allowed to happen.

6. The habits, drills, and routines of government schooling sharply reduce a person's chances of possessing initiative or creativity. Furthermore, the mechanism of why this is so has been well understood for centuries.

7. Teachers are paid as specialists but they almost never have any real world experience in their specialties; indeed the low quality of their training has been a scandal for eighty years.

8. A substantial amount of testimony exists from highly regarded scientists like Richard Feynman, the recently deceased Nobel laureate, or Albert Einstein and many others, that scientific discovery is negatively related to the procedures of school science classes.

9. According to research published by Christopher Jencks, the famous sociologist, and others as well, the quality of school which any student attends is a very bad predictor of later success, financial, social, or emotional. On the other hand the quality of family life is a very good predictor. That would seem to indicate a national family policy directly spending on the home, not the school.

10. Children learn fastest and easiest when very young; general intelligence has probably developed as far as it will by the age of four. Children are quite capable of reading and enjoying difficult material by that age, and also capable of performing all the mathematical operations skillfully and with pleasure. Whether kids *should* do these things or not is a matter of philosophy or cultural

tradition, not a course dictated by any scientific knowledge.

11. There is a direct relationship between heavy doses of teaching and detachment from reality with subsequent flights into fantasy. Many students so oppressed lose their links with past and present, present, and future. And the bond with "now" is substantially weakened.

12. Unknown to the public, virtually all famous remedial programs have failed. Programs like Title I/Chapter I survive by the goodwill of political allies, not by results.

13. There is no credible evidence that racial mixing has any positive effect on student performance, but a large body of suggestive data is emerging that confining one group of children with children of a dominant culture does harm to the smaller group.

14. Forced busing has accelerated the disintegration of minority neighborhoods without any visible academic benefit as trade-off.

15. There is no reason to believe that any existing educational technology can significantly improve intellectual performance; on the contrary, to the extent that machines establish the goals and work schedules, ask the questions and monitor the performances, the already catastrophic passivity and indifference created by schooling only increases.

16. There is no body of knowledge inaccessible to a motivated elementary student. The sequences of development we use are hardly the product of "science," but instead are legacies of unstable men like Pestalozzi and Froebel, and the military governments from which we imported them.

17. Delinquent behavior is a direct reaction to the structure of schooling. It is much worse than the press has reported because all urban school districts conspire to suppress its prevalence. Teach-

ers who insist on justice on behalf of pupils and parents are most frequently intimidated into silence.

18. The rituals of schooling remove flexibility from the mind — that characteristic vital in adjusting to different situations. Schools strive for uniformity in a world increasingly less uniform.

19. Teacher-training courses are widely held in contempt by practicing teachers as well as by the general public because research has consistently failed to provide guidance to best practice.

20. Schools create and maintain a caste system, separating children according to irrelevant parameters. Poor, working class, middle class and upper middle class kids are constantly made aware of alleged differences among themselves by the use of methods not called for by the task at hand.

21. Efforts to draw a child out of his culture or his social class has an immediate effect on his family relationships, friendships, and the stability of his self-image.

Well, there you have them: nine assumptions and twenty-one assertions I think can be documented well enough to call facts. How are we all as a society going to get to a better place in schools than the one we've gotten to at the moment? The only way I can see after spending thirty-five years in and around the institution (fifty-three if I count my own time as a student) is to put full choice squarely back into the hands of parents, let the marketplace redefine schooling, and encourage the development of as many styles of schooling as there are human dreams. Let people, not bureaucrats, work out their own destinies. That's what made us a great country in the first place.

School Books and the Hidden Curriculum

"Stop what you're doing!"

"That is wrong!"

"Do it my way!"

Those cries make up the familiar diatribe of schooling and school books are set up to teach obedience to it. School books lend themselves to testing in very cash-profitable ways, but these are ways which ultimately destroy the ability to read in many, and the educational possibilities of reading in most. Let me give you a way to prove that to yourself.

Erich Maria Remarque's *All Quiet On The Western Front* is one of the great books of this century, available in just about every library in the land, and in school editions, too. As fine a work of art as it is, it's an easy book to read as far as diction and syntax are concerned, being cast in the idiom of German teenagers and young men and translated into the idiom of our own young. Try this simple test on a room full of the best readers you can find: ask them to read the first twenty pages closely and to take notes on anything they think is important. Now have them close the book and using their notes answer this question: "What is the name of the soldier telling the story?" Let me guarantee you that less than ten percent of your subjects will be able to give the name even though the narrator clearly identifies himself. I said ten percent, but I'll be surprised if anyone is able to make the identification. Why is that?

Standardized reading tests never ask such questions — why should a nobody's name have much importance after all? People like that are interchangeable. So the reading drills teachers impose seldom ask for names either. It doesn't take long before a trained reader can't even see information that doesn't fall into the few categories of "valuable" skills which reading tests wallow in.

Not convinced? Here's a bolder scene from the same book, same twenty pages. The second scene of *All Quiet* takes place on the toilet, that ought to be pretty memorable, right? Soldiers have moved their individual potties out of the latrine building so they can watch the battles on land and air above them and in the next field. That's as striking a visual image as you can imagine, isn't it?

Now ask your readers who customarily star on reading exams about the second scene. No matter how you put the question you will discover that only a few, if any, have the vaguest idea the men have taken their toilet outdoors. Not one of my students in fifteen years of asking figured that out — in the face of the well-known teenage appetite for vulgarity. They don't visualize when they read — a century of pseudo-scientific reading instruction which fragments reading into sentences and paragraphs and multiple choice questions and all the rest has destroyed the common ability to bring verbal abstractions down to mental images. A mother reading to her children can often read fluently without formal phonics training or whole word training. But most trained readers can't understand what they read very well. It might be worth your while to reflect on the mechanisms that make this so. Skill with complex reading material was almost universal in colonial days but it became much less so after reading was systematically taught.

Perhaps you need some more convincing, though. Take the

two question test I just offered, then, and enlarge it to ten questions by yourself. The method is this: create questions of sensual detail — colors, smells, sights, etc. — from the first section of *All Quiet*, and perhaps questions of motivation, too. For example, ask what color the boots were that were stolen from the dying man in the field hospital, or how the cook was tricked out of a double ration of beans and sausage. Let the kids read the first twenty pages, then answer your questions open book, using any notes they've taken, in, say, fifteen minutes. If sixty is a passing score, don't expect more than one kid in ten to be able to pass it, even "open book." Trained readers are unable to see what is right beneath their noses. School books, school methods, and school tests do that to kids. The social universe of schooling simply exists for a different purpose than to educate no matter what you've been taught to think otherwise. Although many individual teachers have talent and many try desperately to be "educators," the structure of schools and school books defeat them.

Schools teach a hidden curriculum in mortal combat with the whole educational tradition libraries represent. I'm going to try to illustrate that from history as it is reflected in books for children — "school books" we might call them.

A famous book has had a great deal to do with schools as we know them, and with school books. You most probably consider Plato's *Republic* as an ancient curiosity, but is it not exceedingly strange then that this work is "required reading" in every elite college in the Western world, and in many common colleges as well? Indeed, the private school Plato founded in 385 B.C. to teach the lessons of the book remained in continuous existence for nearly a thousand years. When it closed, those lessons were taught by the higher bureaucracy of the Christian Church, and by Charlemagne, William the Conqueror, Erasmus, and most of the other major forces on the Western stage right down to the present day. Bertrand Russell said that the Communist revolution of 1917 deliberately followed the blueprint of Plato's *Republic*. The Ayatollah Khomeinei's Iran was, by his own acknowledgment, partially an attempt to realize his lifelong ambition to create an Islamic Republic after the example of Plato. No seminar in political science at Harvard treats Plato as a dead issue, perhaps we shouldn't either.

In his *Republic*, Plato's ruling class understands that central control of a state depends upon controlling myths which teach values. State dominance of the contents of imagination must begin in childhood if it is to be dependable, hence Plato's antagonism to family life, which competes with the state by offering myths of its own. Following Plato, rulers throughout history attempted to control myth-making, but met with spotty results because of the absence of any reliable mechanism of effective centralization. The will was there but the technology was lacking.

Rapid development of city life after the American Revolution coincided with the creation of transportation/ communications technology of impressive magnitude to tip the balance, however. After 1850, managing the national imagination became possible. Select universities taught the sons of our elite how myths work to shape social attitudes. But without a social machinery of centralized compulsory schooling, effective control danced out of reach, and American schooling for the first 230 years of our history was local, entrepreneurial, and astonishingly various. No one logic of schooling dominated. There were dozens of ways to grow up right.

The variety of forms in public and private schooling, the abundance of strong natural families who provided homeschooling for a large fraction of the population, the lack of a universal state church except in New England (where the state church, Congregationalism, discouraged centralized tendencies!), and the independence of local writers, journalists, and balladeers — all these factors conspired to deny secular authorities access to the collective consciousness of children. They barred the way, as it were, to any central management's shaping a "planned" society by careful selection of the contents of youthful imagination.

But a combination of historical forces defeated these defenses around the middle of the nineteenth century, principal among these forces being the public horror at waves of Catholic immigration from Ireland. These were welcomed by manufacturers and real estate speculators for the prospect of cheap labor and Western settlement they promised, but feared, too, because the startling Communist revolutions of 1848 made working class groups, especially those from an alien religious tradition, seem menacing.

The machinery created to subdue this danger was compulsory schooling. Talked about for over 2,000 years, beginning with Plato's *Republic*, this radical invasion of family prerogative became a reality in Boston by unanimous vote of a Know-Nothing legislature, then spread instantly to New York and elsewhere. For the first time in history it was possible to realistically contemplate a society without parents.

The parentless society could not be achieved all at once, but it could be approached gradually by filling childish minds with state-approved myths leading in that direction — tales of superior children who willingly attached themselves to a career ideal much grander. The way to this end had been opened by teachings of certain evangelical religions which state flatly that children are only loaned to parents by God. The famous *New England Primer,* America's favorite textbook for 250 years and the bestselling book in American history, openly instructed the young to remember they did not belong to their parents. From that point of abstraction it is a simple step to substituting "the state" in place of "God" as owner of title.

"The old family is dead," declared John Dewey in 1932, proclaiming, he thought, the final victory of state institutions over natural families. It was time for what he called "corporate individualism." The "opportunities, choices and actions of individuals" according to Dewey, "are more and more defined by corporate associations, tightly or loosely organized." Dewey saw a sharp divide between a past where family enterprise and individual effort were the main agencies of personal definition, and a future where institutions would do that better.

I'm going to track the role of school books in helping to create this new state of mind in American children. The stages of evolution this new consciousness went through occupy only a few decades around the turn of the twentieth century. During that time the changing themes of children's books provide us with a sensitive barometer charting the decline of family feeling and personal originality as American values.

These changes were neither natural nor accidental; they were carefully planned and the record of that planning is set down in detail in the minutes of the Boston School Committee, the annual reports of the Children's Aid Society, the records of tent Chautauqua, and in many other corporate associations imbued with the spirit of Plato. After the Boston School Committee sold its compulsory education scheme, the course children's books took was preordained.

I'll start with death as a subject of discussion because that event is universal and profound. If you hang around schools you know death isn't something we ever talk about, acknowledge, or investigate closely. Much of the distaste for aging and aged people found in our culture starts with this failure to acknowledge death as a part of life. But death was a major theme of children's lives and children's books for a very long time. It was only after 1916 that it vanished completely from books, for all the world as if a mysterious conference had been held in which it was mutually agreed children were to be told there is no such thing as grief. Machines don't grieve and neither should people.

A prelude to this sudden banishment can be detected in the removal of evil as a topic between 1900 and 1916 when it ceases totally to exist. These books now argued that there was no such thing as evil, there are only bad attitudes which need not involve God to correct, all being correctable by various scientific "adjustment" therapies. So after evil was dismissed, death died afterwards. What is peculiar in this is that specialists in real books — the people we refer to as "librarians" — recognize how essential the concept of evil is to writing serious literature. It is the rare major writer who does not deal with death and evil. From Rachel Carson to Hannah Arendt's insight on the banality of bureaucratic evil, even nonfiction writers find evil an important landmark of twentieth century history. But not schools, not school books.

The most direct cause of the deletions of evil and death from the imagination of children, and indeed the most direct cause of the anti-family mood sweeping the upper classes at the turn of the century came from a practical philosophy called Positivism. It was a kind of scientific humanism and it made the deepest impression on American academics who travelled to Germany in those years for a scientific education, on American businessmen, politicians, Unitarians, and other practical men of affairs. As broadcast by Frenchman Auguste Comte, it took American society by storm at the very highest levels. Herbert Croly, founder of the magazine *New Republic* (the nod to Plato was intentional), which at the time was one of the most influential journals in the land, had literally been baptized by his parents in the religion of Positivism with chants, white flowing robes, incense, and all. Croly became famous as the architect of Teddy Roosevelt's Progressive platform.

In this way Positivism came to sit at the right hand of political power in America. And it became the undeclared religion of American schooling, just as Horace Mann intended it to be.

Auguste Comte was a childless man, like so many other men who have shaped European and American social policy toward children. A measure of the passion his ideas awoke in his power elite following may be gathered by the fact that his extended stays in the insane asylum at Charenton had no effect on his influence.

Comte's grand vision was a new spiritual power which treated God as an impossible concept. The new God, said Comte, would

be the state. His countryman, Emile Durkheim, the most important sociologist who ever lived, agreed completely. The state would
teach us how to live in the emerging beehive world, a world which
must abandon both true individualism and natural families for a
higher purpose. With this guiding ideal, Positivism set out to create a new world order. Incidentally, the writings of the Positivists
frequently contain that expression "new world order," just as the
new American dollar bill after 1935 did. Considering the immense
influence the Positivist movement had on prominent American
thinkers, leaders in business, government, military, and church, the
absence of any discussion about it from all school book histories
dealing with the period seems a lamentable and peculiar oversight.

Between 1880 and 1920, strict regulation of American society became a leadership imperative. Explanations for this
phenomenon begin once again with the alarming effects of mass
immigration on the morale of American leadership. It is not an
extreme reading of evidence to say genuine panic existed — fear
that ancient ways of distributing wealth and authority might be in
jeopardy.

A striking evidence of this panic is contained in accounts of
academic behavior during the period. To cite only one case, President William Walker of MIT declared in speeches and writings
that the large, close families of immigrants were provoking intolerable racial competition, leading to something he called "racial
suicide" among the so-called Anglo-Saxon races. Between 1900 and
1910 the theme of racial suicide was a common topic in all leading
popular magazines.

This fear of racial suicide was provoked by an unusual "close-ness" of immigrant families. Puritan leaders had always described family intimacy as sacrilegious, favoring family loyalty in its place (for the prosperity loyalty brought in its train). In the large affectionate broods of Irish and Italians, and in their relative indifference to material rewards when compared to the rewards of family life, a mortal threat was perceived.

Comte's Positivist lessons dismissing family as an anachronism then mingled with a widespread hatred of the dangerous cultures of immigration to produce a national agenda of state imposed conformity. The push to this end was motivated by more than just theoretical considerations; violent strikes against management in coal, steel, and railroads signalled that the danger from these people was more than long-range, it was very close at hand.

School books and other texts to sell myths of conformity followed hard on the heels of compulsory schooling. And toward the end of this second phase of mass immigration, another Communist revolution occurred, this time a successful one. At that exact historical moment the compulsory education laws were given teeth. Widely ignored after the initial flush of enthusiasm passed, the laws were now made unavoidable. The power of the state was placed at the disposal of school authorities, and the new mass government schooling institution began with a vengeance to separate children and families, assisted by the creation of many another astonishing new institution to assist in the deconstruction.

Come back with me for a few minutes to the earlier period when we first got government schools to compel our belief. The overnight invention of compulsory schooling in mid-nineteenth century Boston — and the equally radical instant invention of a unique mass-adoption institution — is a sign that something extraordinary was afoot. Both developments coincide with the beginnings of mass immigration, both remove children from parents in unprecedented ways, both are absolutely unopposed politically, and neither is preceded by much public announcement or debate. None, indeed, in the case of adoption.

And beginning around the year 1850, a remarkable apparatus of surveillance and regulation was put into place, a social machine that was Calvin's dream of constant scrutiny come true. Though vigorously opposed by the South, after the Civil War removed the social dialectic between North and South the road was clear for continuous development and refinement in the arena of state oversight of private lives. Some of the new institutions worth noting are: secret national police forces; the invention of courts expressly for children, where due process rights and the rights of defendants to confront accusers are removed; the appearance of a national tax system designed to provide intimate details of family life to authorities; a national elevation of the "expert" scholar to star status by travelling tent shows in every state; a new allegiance to "research" universities after the Prussian model which replaced "teaching" universities; and the sudden appearance of a national research hospital system, in which hospital care was aggressively sold as the superior successor to home-style sick care or home-style birthing. Of course, the diamond in this crown of state scrutiny and control was compulsory schooling.

It was a social revolution without precedent in history, and it happened only yesterday. Not in any of its particulars was it popularly sought nor was it even democratically discussed. Indeed the roots of the movement, philosophically, were not European at all, but Egyptian in concept — reaching through these new state institutions toward a vision of society as well-regulated and predictable, like the stones and courses in an Egyptian pyramid. It was a new world order and when its progress seemed irrevocable it was triumphantly announced on the back of the new dollar bill of 1935, which featured an Egyptian pyramid, a most appropriate symbol for the Positivistic world of the future.

Without explanation or warning, timeless cultural myths disappeared from children's books between 1890 and 1920, replaced by new synthetic myths children were encouraged to accept. Before we get into more specifics of this change (we've already touched on the removal of death and evil as themes) the very suddenness of change warrants careful reflection. Any abrupt departure from tradition in the content of children's books is so economically risky it just couldn't happen unless it was a collective industry decision made at the highest levels; and such a decision could not by its nature be based on marketing considerations, but had to be reached through a much different logic. In the thirty-year period in question, our textbook industry suddenly became a creator of values, not a reflector of them; only the monopolistic nature of school publishing allowed this transformation.

Until 1875, about three quarters of all titles for children dealt with some perspective on the span of life, birth to death, and what might be beyond it. But by 1915 that idea was gone. Past and future disappeared from these books; past meant family life and traditional thinking; future speculations awakened the appetite for free will choices. Neither of these things was going to be encouraged.

Positivism advised that children should be relieved of concern with the future. The need to do God's will was judged an unpatriotic superstition because it introduced the idea of a higher power against which decisions of the state might be appealed.

Another dramatic leap in the content of children's books involved the downgrading of cultural communities. From the seventeenth to the end of the nineteenth centuries, the strengths thought to be derived from stable community life were an important part of the texture of schooling and school books, but toward the end of the nineteenth century a distinctly new note was heard, the note of "self" as opposed to "community" and "family." With this change protagonists became fully independent of Mother and Father. The master of these tales was Horatio Alger, the bestselling author in American history. Alger's more than 100 titles are family and community free. His plucky boys have no need for family or for communal affirmation; they work for themselves and for the recognition of outside authorities.

Needs that are now showcased for the young are the so-called "expressive" needs: playing, joy, "self-actualizing," the pleasure of winning possessions. By the start of the twentieth century a solid majority of children's books focused on the individual child freed from the web of family and community. In these texts children are tempted to divide their own interests from those of their families, their ethnic cultures, and their communities by the promise of personal gain.

Another important change came from the decline of

old-fashioned self-reliant individualism. From 1796 to 1855, only eighteen percent of all children's titles were constructed around the idea of conformity, but by 1896 the emphasis on conformity had tripled. The termination of individuality as a value was, as I mentioned before, made possible largely by the defeat of the South in this period.

The "new" individualism John Dewey talked about wasn't really individualism at all except in appearances. It encouraged its followers to self-start and to proceed on what appeared to be a course independent of the past, but that was merely a therapeutic strategy; as Horace Mann had advocated the use of Bibles in school to throw the Christian sects off the track of what was really going on, so, too, the brave show of independence in children's texts always led toward a centrally designed social goal. There were no exceptions.

Free will in Dewey's "new individualism" is a perception, not an actuality. You feel that you have it, but the outside world perceives you are doing exactly what everyone else is doing. George Orwell illustrated the significance of this in *1984* when Winston Smith is compelled, seemingly of his own free will, to denounce his love, transferring his affection from her to Big Brother. That was Orwell's dramatization of what he saw happening all around him — in a world where school books were strangling real books, and children were being discouraged from reading well by schools. Why should reading skill be a priority of schooling? Readers have access to original points of view; they have an inner life into which the state has difficulty penetrating.

But in the new system social engineers got the best of both worlds: a large measure of control without those being controlled realizing it. No rebellions possible then, only dysfunctional behaviors like suicide, drug addiction, violence, and neurosis. These, because disorganized, were only nuisances compared to what might come about from a race of original thinkers created by independent reading.

One of the most violent myths through children's books was the one which replaced hard work as the goal of book characters with something the books called "education." Let me provide a possible explanation for that drawn from economic developments of the period. The national economy by the end of the nineteenth century had largely eliminated free enterprise and competition from its internal workings. The International Harvester Corporation was well on its way to convincing government the day of the small farmer was over and that the demise of residual sentimentality in this regard must be artificially hastened. Small competitive manufacturing, local opportunities, transportation companies, and a host of other commercial possibilities for the little man were being foreclosed rapidly by political control large corporations exercised over the marketplace. The professions, long an outlet for singular talent and personal intensity, were rapidly brought under control of exclusive licensing procedures preempted by the university's managerial class.

In an economy increasingly unable to provide satisfying work to more than a fraction of its citizens, reservation of children away from the world of work became more than just an aesthetic preference; it was a bulwark against rebellion. Most of the new machine jobs and symbol-manipulation jobs were intentionally designed to be "worker-proof," and so could have been done easily by children. Thus it became necessary to find a way for the young to be prevented from taking them.

In spite of the successful ancient practice of children and adults working side by side as an efficient and humane way to socialize the young, the term "child labor" began to appear in book as condemnation; upper-class vigilantes formed associations to harass poor and working class families who persisted in these traditional ways. Children were encouraged to avoid work as long as possible, replacing it with nonspecific benefits of schooling.

An index of the power of the new myths was their ability to suppress landmarks of spectacular achievement among America's working children, children who later distinguished themselves intellectually and materially. The experience of young Benjamin Franklin, working full-time at age ten by his own choice, proved a continual embarrassment to the child-labor gang, an embarrassment eventually managed by reducing prosperous Ben Franklin to the status of a "poor boy" so that it seemed he had no choice but to work. And the experience of Andrew Carnegie moving from penury to enormous wealth as a working teenager as well as the histories of many another unschooled success were skillfully disguised. Nowhere in children's literature after 1916 can be heard the well-documented success record of working children, a record which challenges the case for keeping children idle and passive.

In the new literature, families are portrayed as good-natured dormitory arrangements, even as manager-employee relationships, but they are never portrayed as the core of life's meaning; private goals are pursued through social institutions, not through family efforts. Significant family undertakings, like starting a farm or a business, are rare in the new world of school books, as rare as is death, evil, self-schooling, the importance of ethnic culture, tales of the ways strong families interact with each other, or the successes of hard working children.

Thus, though unstated and unannounced, lessons about family life, personality, career, and many other chapters in the passage from child to adult were mythologized anew and quietly showcased in the theater of school books. From World War One onwards the curriculum of these books was increasingly selfish, yet at the same time collective. It was anti-family, anti-community, and antireligious. Hardly anybody was aware of what it was saying or where it was leading. John Dewey knew, I think, but hardly anybody noticed. And here we are.

Horatio Alger's Country: The Mysterious Origins of American Adoption

The Horatio Alger theme was a joy and a solace. It showed that a young man who was too good to be true was also bound to be successful. . . . Alger was one of the men who all but effaced the New England tradition, for he vulgarized Emerson's Self-Reliance *and turned into a laughingstock Longfellow's* Excelsior *and* The Psalm of Life. *He made virtue and purity odious.*
— *Van Wyck Brooks*

Some years ago, never mind how long precisely, I thought I might sail around in some research libraries and see what caused the curious institution of sealed-record adoption to come about. Substitute child care is only a minor monument of a culture, of course, yet I could not shake my obsession with the puzzle. Why had our particular society seen fit to obliterate the historical identity of adopted children and no land before us? And why in the twentieth century and not before?

Eventually I stumbled on some answers, but along the way such mysteries were encountered the original question about adoption came to appear too modest. After a time adoption faded in my mind as a self-contained institution. I came to see adoption as only one bright thread in a vast Bayeaux tapestry illuminating a Viking invasion of the American family. On the track of a weasel I ran into Fenris Wolf.

I'll ask you to go back with me to the year 1843 when the American Republican party was established in New York City, an outfit whose platform stressed opposition to voting and office-holding privileges for Catholics and foreigners. This event is sometimes used as a signpost to mark the start of the hundred-year-long outpouring of American "nativism" that changed the fare of every American institution and ended in a paroxysm of orthodoxy.

Of course it's possible to find a much earlier flaring of American nativism that suggests dislike of the unorthodox foreigner is rooted deeply in the blood that brought our nationhood about:

- 18 June, 1798. The Naturalization Act changed from five to fourteen years the period of residence required for admission to full citizenship.
- 25 June, 1798. The Alien Act authorized the President to order out of the U.S. all aliens regarded as dangerous to the public peace and safety, or suspected of "secret inclinations."
- 6 July, 1798. The Alien Enemies Act authorized the President, in time of declared war, to arrest, imprison, or banish aliens subject to an enemy power.
- 14 July, 1798. The Sedition Act made it a high misdemeanor to prevent a federal officer from performing his duty to attempt "unlawful assembly."

The mechanisms set in public motion in 1798 and 1843, like the little mill of the fairy tale, are still grinding salt no matter how many masks and costumes they've donned in the interim.

It will be useful before proceeding to reflect a minute on the state of the nation in 1843. We were within a few decades of swallowing the whole continental mass between the two oceans, and all of this geometrical expansion and multiplication from Jamestown, Boston, New York, and Philadelphia had been accomplished by Anglo-Normans from a relatively small strip of southeastern England where, oddly enough, the towns of Boston and New York are but eight miles apart. There had been minor supplemental migrations to be sure but by 1840 only 25,000 practicing Catholics intruded into a mass of 17,000,000 Protestants, and over a quarter of the entire population was directly descended from the 4,000 Puritan families known to have debarked in New England between 1620 and 1700. America was a family affair for its first 230 years or more. If you make that reality vivid in your imagination, the "why" and "how" and "who" of adoption, otherwise a treacherous morass of obscure names and meetings, will begin to make sense.

Many mystifying questions about the family as an American institution will benefit from a close examination of family life in England in the zone from London south and across to Cambridge University. By 1843 North America had emerged as a forge and intensifier for Anglo-Norman traits, values, habits, humors, and philosophies that survived the English Reformation, but particularly for a regional code from that particular section. This is a zone which includes quaint villages, a zone still pagan a full hundred years after the rest of the island had Christianized. That's more important than it first appears. The spiritual bellows of the American forge was a mixture of Old Norse pragmatism, Martin Luther mysticism and passion, John Calvin legalism and organization, and the dear-eyed civilities of Anglicanism, but a pagan heart and mind

ran the works and the Christian holiday of Christmas was region-
ally suppressed through New England until well into the nineteenth
century.

The philosophical engine, however, was another matter entirely. It had been built by a peculiar group of rational utopians
known as Cambridge Platonists, a spirited group tracing its intellectual provenance back through the Humanists of the Renaissance
to Charlemagne, then back further through St. Augustine to Marcus
Aurelius and the Stoics, and finally back to the master, Plato himself, especially to his vision of the perfect state drawn in *The Republic* and *Laws.*

The early American experiment was purely an Anglo-Norman
adventure, self-consciously Anglo-Norman among the upper
classes, but there was hardly need for others to be self-conscious
since the cultural unity of the population was nearly universal. That
unified structure of the U.S. was trembling by 1843. A threat from
the original Christianity of Europe was nearly at hand. In Lyons,
France, in 1822 a papal plan for Roman Catholic missions to the
United States had been formulated, some 200 years after the nation's
settlement. This mission was placed under the direction of an en-
tity known as The Society for the Propagation of the Faith; in
Vienna seven years later a group called the Leopold Association
was given a similar mission: bring Catholicism to the United States.
The Catholics were coming.

The effect on the unified society of the U.S. was quick and
violent; trouble antedated actual Catholic descent on these shores
by over a decade. It was as if the specter of Anglo-Saxon America
being breached by aliens was in itself enough to spoil Utopia. Left
to their solitude, the English had driven back and dominated the

Indian race, had captured, sequestered, and set to useful labor the black race. These peoples had not the power or sophistication to resist mental colonization any better than they could resist physical colonization it seemed. They required alert surveillance but were otherwise no cause for concern.

But long English experience with other white peoples foretold there would be no easy mastery of spirit, however speedily they might be otherwise brought to heel. The Irish had provided a long, unpleasant experience for Albion, the Spanish, and French, too. Serious trouble was certainly at hand. It was time for serious action to combat it.

On August 11, 1834, the Ursaline Convent in Boston was burned to the ground. In the New York elections of 1844 an American Republican nativist mayor was elected who pledged to force Catholic schoolchildren to read the King James version of the Bible; in May and July of 1844 armed attacks on Catholics were launched in Philadelphia, and there in the next year the Native American party was formed and held its national convention. Eastern pulpits rang with denunciations of Catholicism by Reverend Lyman Beecher, of the famous Beecher clan, and news stalls hawked anti-Catholic writings of equally famous inventor Samuel F. B. Morse. A penny would buy you *Priestcraft Unmasked*, another coin, Rebecca Reed's sexy stories of life behind convent walls.

While these things were happening there really weren't very many actual Catholics around — not yet. But something else was happening in these years that was to have much greater effect on the destiny of our national family policy than the sharing of this land with Celts, Latins, and Slavs. What was happening everywhere, even in the most orthodox Calvinist strongholds like Yale and Princeton, was the disintegration of Protestant Christianity.

The causes were immensely complex, perhaps the isolation of the New World from theological competition, perhaps the limitless prosperity and boundless spaces providing world and time for too much experimentation — these things certainly had something to do with the falling away in the churches. But something more deliberate was gnawing away at conventional piety. Protestant Christianity was being attacked from within by a culture of ethical rationality masquerading as a religion. The inspiration, the immediate vision guiding this movement, was from Voltaire, Diderot, Rousseau, and the French Enlightenment, and the remote antecedents from Italy and Greece of classical times, but all by way of contemporary utopian developments in Germany and France.

In the United States this force was called Unitarianism; its central headquarters, Boston. It was more a method than a creed. In essence it said, "You can believe pretty much what you want, as long as you are ethically orthodox." The trick about Unitarianism, and all the many "Unity" variations of it which sprung up, was that although the dead parent may have been religious, the descendant form was almost entirely ethical. In shapes like Ethical Culture, even Christian religious ancestry was denied, in some uncanny fashion it was as if the Old Norse religion had been reborn.

Essentially these are conjunctions of a different kind of faithful — those who prefer to ignore the mysterious origin of life and other non-verifiable matters like spiritual destiny and concentrate on the here and now. Underneath a physical legacy of church architecture and perhaps an organ and flowers most of the new sermons were exhortations to good conduct — like calls for spirited performance that pass around a baseball infield. The main beliefs are two: the everyday should be man's main concern; the individual is sovereign. This is a far cry from traditional Christian emphasis on man's dependency on God, which stresses this life mainly as a preparation for the afterlife to come, and it is a long distance, too, from the New Testament injunction to love one another. Under all ethical and rational trappings, the new religion — still calling itself Christianity — was the religion of a feudal society of warriors, not unlike Viking society had been.

When eminent revivalist Charles Finney arrived in Boston in 1843, Lyman Beecher said to him, "The Unitarians have destroyed the foundations of Christianity. The people are all afloat. You can take nothing for granted about what they believe, but must begin at the very beginning." Thirty years later Finney elaborated. "It is extremely difficult to make religious truths lodge in people's minds because the influence of Unitarian teaching has been to lead them to call into question the principal doctrines of the Bible. They deny almost everything and affirm almost nothing."

Unitarianism seemed to have a great deal in common with the Deist view of Washington and Jefferson and with the clear statements of Tom Paine in his *Rights of Man* and *Age of Reason* tracts. It was reform-minded and had a rational agenda that trusted man to be able to solve his own problems without divine assistance. Unlike traditional Christianity, it assumed man was inherently good, infinitely perfectible; the idea of an evil nature to be mastered, or The Fall from a once lofty state were unacceptable to the new dogma. All could be turned to the best, and this was the best of all possible worlds. In fact it was the perfect theological companion for Auguste Comte's philosophical Positivism which came out of France in the same period. The philosophy of Positivism only admitted knowledge gained by the methods of science as real, just as Unitarianism reasoned the miraculous element out of the gospel by stating the leprosy Jesus healed was presumably a skin disease, and explained the falling of the wind at Jesus' command as a natural subsidence, misinterpreted as miraculous by the disciples.

The agenda of Unitarianism bore more than a passing similarity to the ambitions of Adam Weishaupt and his society of fabulous Illuminati that sprang up at the University of Ingolstadt in Germany in 1776 — the finest minds and subtlest sensibilities working on secrets that kept men from being gods. Weishaupt's goals, the awesome confidence of the French *Encyclopedia*, the god-like path seemingly followed by America's great fraternity of Freemasons like Benjamin Franklin, Alexander Hamilton, and all the others — all these seemed in silent partnership with the Unitarian message that man was the measure of all things.

Weishaupt's Illuminati were a subject of excited drawing room discussion in Boston and New York, Baltimore and Philadelphia at about the time of the rise of Unitarianism in 1819-1820 because twenty-one-year-old Mary Shelley's new novel, *Frankenstein, or the Modern Prometheus*, had been published just the year before (1818) and its themes were on everybody's lips, everybody of culture at least. Dr. Frankenstein, a young medical student at the University of Ingolstadt, animates a soulless monster made out of corpses by means of galvanism. Family-less, unable to find love and sympathy, the monster ultimately turns to dreadful retribution on Frankenstein for usurping the Creator's prerogatives. Miss Shelley seemed to be saying there were limits beyond which science should not reach.

Titillating to be sure, but by 1820 hers was a minority position in the United States. Most influential men and women believed then as President Eliot of Harvard did a hundred years later when he said about Christ and the Bible, "We no longer depend for salvation upon either a man or a book. Men help us; books help us; but back of all stands our divine reason." The presidents of Harvard were called by Thomas Carlyle "the Unitarian popes."

The Protestant world of the United States received two shocks in the first and second quarters of the nineteenth century. The first arose dynamically from events and associations of the French Enlightenment which culminated in a stupendous social revolution. It was a new dialectical rationalism that questioned everything, undermining all the foundations of the old order, one of which was the hegemony of the family institution. The control structure of this new way of seeing masqueraded, in part, as a religion of rationality, aiming to bring about a "unitarian" world. The second shock came from an unprecedented Catholic invasion of the new world through immigration, defiling the purity of what for centuries had been the laboratory of Calvinism and Anglo-Norman style. Inside of thirty years the Protestant world was turned upside down and inside out, not least by the scramble among powerful Protestant families to gather fortunes disposing of millions of new souls — as cheap labor in factories, on railroads, as servants, and as settlers in a real estate boom of such magnitude it cleansed the country of its original native population in fifty years, leaving it permanently homeless. Out of this bewildering chaos came the modern world's first adoption law.

Midwives of this new instrument of population control were many, but among those who deserve a prominent place is the name of Fanny Wright, a major figure in nineteenth century history whose proper biographer is yet to appear. When this wealthy orphan came to the U.S. in 1824, she was not yet thirty but had authored two books and a play, including a thoroughly worked out philosophy of scientific materialism based on the principles of Epicurus. Arm-in-arm with her close friend the Marquis de Lafayette she arrived at Thomas Jefferson's door and became his house guest. There, in a meeting with James Madison, Jefferson, and Lafayette she presented a plan for the emancipation of black slaves and their resettlement in Africa. As a test of her plan Fanny purchased a quantity of black slaves, placed them on a vast estate she owned in Tennessee, trained them in domestic husbandry, and had them resettled at her own expense in Haiti. Were it not for the unfortunate fact that the practice of free love she advocated for her employees aroused mortal animosity in her Tennessee neighbors, the experiment would have been repeated.

In a short time, together with Robert Owen, she founded the communal colony of New Harmony in Indiana. The year was 1825 and you will note that Fanny had been in this part of the world only a year. In later years, Owen acknowledged that it was Fanny Wright's driving energy that kept his famous utopian enterprise going. Fanny preached constantly for birth control and equal rights for women, and just as constantly she preached against marriage, religion, and home education. Fanny's wit, beauty, and fiery ideas were soon items of conversation in every drawing room of nineteenth century America.

Like most freethinkers of early nineteenth century Europe, Frances Wright was deeply impressed by mathematical arguments, stemming from Malthus, that strict restraint in procreation was necessary to avoid population disaster. When she joined with Owens and Thomas Skidmore to found the Workingman's Party in New York City and Philadelphia in 1829 — a party which, incidentally, was immediately successful and gained the balance of power in the latter city — she worked her family ideas into a new system of child-care, insisting they be adopted in the platform of the party.

Because these ideas destroyed the Workingman's Party, and because they provide us with the beginnings of a continuous thread from Frances Wright in 1829 through the Know-Nothing legislatures in Massachusetts a little more than two decades later, through the establishment of Children's Court in Chicago in 1899, through the settlement houses of New York, the establishment of compulsory education, the rise of social work as a profession in the years before World War I, through the sealing of adoption records in Minnesota in 1917, and right into the modern world of child care experts, daycare, no-fault divorces, and shared custody parenting — because these ideas of the remarkably attractive and able Fanny Wright are so very potent and germane to our own reality today — they bear close attention:

What Fanny said was, "The care and education of all children should be placed under the guardianship of the state. Children should be removed from their parents at an early age. It is preferable they be placed in state-operated boarding schools."

This was no Madam LaFarge, but a brilliant, dominant soul as comfortable as Thomas Jefferson's house guest as she was founding successful political parties, writing books and plays, or setting up colonies in Haiti. It is a curious failure of popular history that this influential woman has remained a cipher.

She was denounced frequently as an infidel bent on destroying the family. A year after its founding the Workingman's Party repudiated state guardianship of children; shortly afterwards the party disappeared. Fanny eventually left this country, but her idea, clothed with the melody of her lovely voice and exhilarating presence, stayed behind. Plato may have said it first, and Rousseau emphasized his own statement that parents are unnecessary in successful child-rearing by giving away his own children, but what could compare in impact to a beautiful young woman of wealth, taste, and intelligence arguing such a case just a few feet away? Miss Wright's blueprint gained powerful allies.

Fanny saw compulsory education as an intermediary stage in achieving a uniform, rationally organized, infinitely perfectible synthetic family. The anti-family aspects of influential contemporary treatises like Johann Fichte's *Complete Theory of Knowledge* and the ever-present *eminence grise* of Hobbes and his Leviathan state, of which Napoleon had almost served as Prometheus, are strewn over the landscape in abundance for those who care to look. In all the utopian visions, compulsory education as an institution figures prominently — and it was known to be one of the calling cards of Freemasonry in the attempts of that body to influence American politics.

In the twenty-year period from 1829, when the Workingman's Party was founded, to 1849, when a clandestine organization that had called itself The Order of the Star-Spangled Banner surfaced as the Know-Nothing Party, the underpinnings of American public school compulsion were set in place. In the same year Mary Shelley published *Frankenstein,* infant schools were introduced into Boston and spread quickly to New York, as quickly as if those cities had been a mere eight miles apart.

External events also transpired during that brief period that helped select the course of U.S. family policy. Alien cultural groups were impinging upon our territorial integrity: an organization of South American states met in Panama under Bolivar to discuss hemispheric unity; Mexico and Cuba continued to be thought of as daggers poised at our throat; with alarm it was noted that in Mexican Texas and Florida there was indiscriminate mixing of Anglo-Saxon and Spanish cultures. It was decided our manifest destiny did not include hybridizing with the Spanish.

Slave insurrections from 1832 onwards promised the long term headache that de Tocqueville's books on American democracy had foreseen. Providing for the eventual human tidal wave which would be released by the end of slavery was a part of political thinking even then. But easily the most important precedent set during those years for family policy was Andrew Jackson's establishment of a Bureau of Indian Affairs and the consequent forcible resettlement of the Cherokee Nation and other tribes out of areas where they were inconvenient or offensive to English culture. The indigenous peoples, in place for countless millennia, were removed and dispatched to the barren lands in a kind of "out of

sight, out of mind" gesture. Few precedents for such a radical solution exist in modern human history.

In Worcester v. Georgia, 6 Peters 515, the John Marshall Supreme Court tried to defend the Cherokee Nation from encroach-
ment by Georgia interests, but Jackson was reported to say, "John
Marshall has made his decision, now let him enforce it!" Jackson
pursued a broad policy of extinguishing Indian land titles and re-
moving the Indian population. During his two terms, ninety-four
Indian treaties were concluded including treaties of evacuation with
the Creeks, Choctaw, and Chickasaw. By 1833, only the Cherokee
remained, insisting on their lands. But in December 1835, they were
transported west as well.

This bold policy of social intervention in the community life
of an indigenous people established a tradition of unsentimental
disposition of family policy questions on a basis of rational
self-interest. Perhaps it might be argued that our cultural practice
of transporting African families and disposing them by economic
logic rather than preserving their families intact had already set
the pattern for treating both family and community as dispens-
able. The Elizabethan Poor Laws and Enclosure had once created
a class of impermanent, dependent poor in England — a base on
which every great industrial fortune now stood. The colonies had
taken signal steps in that direction, but more was needed in the
way of making the lower and middle classes rootless, too.

It is time to take another look, briefly, at colonial America's
founding families and the historical context out of which they came,
the incredible homogeneity I've already mentioned and those en-

ergetic Scandinavian/North German rootstocks from which they sprang. Germanic contingents had come out of the mist and oak forests again and again between the fifth and eleventh centuries to settle England; their last invasion by Duke William of Normandy produced the English ruling classes for the rest of history. William was fifth in line of descent from Hrolf the Ganger, "the man who walks," so named it is thought because he was too big to sit on a horse. Perhaps, however, like the Norse god, Thor, whom he worshipped, he simply preferred to walk.

Duke William paid homage to Odin, Thor, Tiw, Frigga, and the other Aesir — although living in northern France he was a Norseman and as such part of a Norse culture. Descriptions of Nordic behavior are consistent from Tacitus all the way to writers of fifteenth century travel memoirs, and much confirmation is available from stunning archaeological finds in Scandinavia where climate assists wonderfully in preserving old flesh and stale bread across the aeons.

Some discoveries about the Nordic personality will be useful as we track their descendants down through the centuries and on into Harvard, the space program, and the history of family life on these shores.

In the first place, the northmen seemed to have always been intensely independent, even of each other. They practiced solitary burial and liked to keep their domiciles well-spaced. The love for independence, however, should not be confused with an admiration for the principle of independence, far from it; their slave and serf classes were large.

Even from pre-Christian times they appear to have been fearless, driven by the spirits of pride, greed, and curiosity to endure formidable amounts of pain and discomfort without complaint. This same mixed spirit caused them to range more widely than any culture of record on the planet — deep into Asia, south to Africa, west to the Americas. The extent of their American excursions still remains to be determined; they were never builders and so left no monuments. At least this much is known. They were here 500 years before any other European was known to have been, and perhaps they were here long before that.

The pagan religion they practiced is unlike any on record in the extent of its materialism, its violent energy, and its suspicion of everyone and every human situation. Nobody could be trusted, nothing is really sacred because all is merely a mechanical by-product of heat and cold, and everything on earth and in heaven is doomed to destruction in a mighty conflagration called Ragnarok. Power is respected, weakness held in contempt, the powerless are reviled and are every man's resource to exploit. When Thor is befriended by a kindly giant who carries his baggage and boards him for the night in his own home, the Norse god thinks nothing of bashing out his host's brains while he sleeps. Dead, it will be easier to steal his goods. These ethics are the ethics of a pirate culture and they remained consistent over thousands of years. Their love of war is too well-known to require elaboration, but less well-known is the ambiguity these tribes felt toward strong leadership. Sabotaging a strong leader was as common an occurrence as was hero worship; both conditions alternated in the divided soul of the Germanic.

The great material success of the northern peoples is thus not hard to account. They were highly adaptable and free of ethics, which meant they could adjust to foreign places and languages with great ease. They were not burdened with sentimental traditions as so many of the peoples with whom they came into conflict. Nothing proved that more than the blood-price — a kinsman killed by treachery was never the subject of vengeance if the killer could produce cash to pay for the life taken. This custom among Scandinavians and Saxons spared them many internecine squabbles but also emphasized the importance of law-courts to settle disputes. Arabs noted with disgust that unlike Islamic blood-price customs — which might only be invoked if the death had been accidental — these people applied blood-price indiscriminately. Living as though no life was irreplaceable except one's own had obvious advantages. And led to distinctive shapes of human society.

Nordic areas are the birthplace of the corporation mind. Those Hanseatic cities which served as a forge of modern business architecture in the twelfth century were the result of a thousand years of profitable business and trade by the north with far-flung parts of the world. And the best business of all was trading in lives — "personnel services" one might say. From 600 to 1000 A.D., Vikings were the principal slave traders of Europe and the Near East, just as their English descendants were the principal slave traders of the world from the fifteenth to the eighteenth century. This was the externalization of their domestic custom of maintaining huge serf and slave classes in the homelands. Near the top of the pyramid stood a much smaller number of craftsmen and peasants and at the very pinnacle stood a small, elect, aristocratic warrior class.

Two last characteristics of our original colonial heritage bear mention. Norsemen and Saxons were passionately addicted to technology and clockwork organization; their quick genius recognized very early the advantages conferred by machines. The longship was the best hit-and-run profit-making machine of its time, and it is appropriate that England's own future heyday was contingent on the development of a high-tech battle fleet.

Coupled with canny fascination for machinery was a complementary understanding that making one's own men machine-like was a winning strategy for competing against undisciplined barbarians. It also offered the most efficient control mechanism with the underclasses. And whether applying rigorous discipline to one's own children or to the children of serfs, what was well-understood is that it is many times easier to shape a child than a recalcitrant grown-up.

Frequently travellers to England from Latin countries would remark how cold and distant English parents were with their own children. By the time of the Norman invasion, the custom of sending English children into domestic service with a family far from home was a national custom, uniting every social class in common understanding. The English had discovered how much easier it is to discipline and train a child alone. Stripped of his family, the child will be utterly dependent and fearful because his familiar world has vanished.

Evidence for the cultural idiosyncrasies of Anglo-Saxon child-rearing is abundant and yields remarkably consistent data over a 1,500 year period. Francis Bacon, an important shaper of the modern scientific temper, had a great deal of influence in codifying Anglo-Saxon ambiguity toward intact, loving families. Bacon noted, "Wife and children are impediments to great enterprises. Certainly, the best works and of the greatest merit for the public

Horatio Alger's Country ✦ 151

have proceeded from the unmarried or childless men." He explained this by contending that single men "marry the public" and endow it, rather than their own children. But on the lower levels of society Bacon was not unmindful of the value of seeing to it underlings had wives and children. "Unmarried men are not always the best subjects, for they are light to run away; and almost all fugitives are of that condition." In these words from "Of Marriage and the Single Life" Bacon brackets the contradictory conditions of modern commercial life where families are a requirement of promotion in many industries, yet the reality of family must be avoided in order to compete successfully against others.

Bacon was even more emphatic in his essay "Of Parents and Children" about minimizing the importance of family life. "The perpetuity by generation is common to beasts," he said, agreeing with Martin Luther that marriage and procreation is no divine sacrament but simply a human contract. Bacon's thinking continues, "But memory, merit, and noble works are proper to men." The same love for fame that swims electrically through great Norse sagas, that forms the code of honor of the Teutonic Knights, and underlies our own contemporary lists of distinction is caught neatly in those ten words. He concludes, "Surely a man shall see the noblest works and foundations have proceeded from childless men [seeking] to express the images of their minds."

It's time for us to return to the nineteenth century and join the caucuses of The Order of the Star-Spangled Banner as it plots America's new adoption law. We'll gain admission by murmuring its secret password — "I don't know" — and become

Know-Nothings. But getting to a position where it's possible to understand the potency of such an association in the evolution of American child-rearing requires that several foundational ideas be grasped.

Foremost of these is knowledge of the ongoing conflict between the "true state" of Hobbes, Plato, Bacon and other utopian philosophers, and the "fictitious state" which is an illusory cover for an oligarchy of powerful, long-range families. An analogy to this hidden warfare between what seems and what is is caught in the story of Maelzel's robot Chessplayer, once the darling of great salons, a machine concealing a corrupt dwarf who gave the dead machine the semblance of human insight. From the midget's point-of-view there was great triumph in convincing arrogant drawing rooms that a machine had life, and, conversely, that he did not exist.

Next, it is important to understand that all thinking about what the state might become needs a theory of managed child development. Without any exceptions, state intervention into the privacy of the natural family has been a major part of every European government's tenure for the past 500 years, becoming stronger as we move toward our own time and our own country. And stronger, too, in the North than in the South.

State policy toward family affairs is the first place we need to look to determine why families are collapsing, and state policies always evolve out of philosophical treatises, seldom from human experience or popular preference. Many will be surprised and offended by this statement, assuming that there is no official family policy in the minds of most people. That is quite false, but to discover where such a policy resides requires us to ignore rhetoric and seek out its hiding-holes. No one will be disappointed; it is there.

One rewarding zone to scan is that of American literature. Our two most influential and profitable literary offerings over the past 300 years have been *The New England Primer* (circa 1680) and the works of Horatio Alger — about a hundred books that appeared mostly in the last quarter of the nineteenth century.

First, the *Primer*. More than six million copies are known to have been in print by 1830, and the book was in use until the end of the century, and is read even today. The power of the *Primer* was extensive, its influence immeasurable. Therefore, it is far from a literary exercise to be curious about the contents of this bible of every school child. Well, among other things it told young readers their own parents were merely custodians of their lives, lives held in trust for some greater power. In fact, one of the three signs of true salvation was Adoption — with a capital "A" — into God's own family and out of the child's own. When baby trains first rolled west in 1853 carrying Irish children away from their mothers and fathers the *Primer* was in each child's hands. It justified what was happening so the radical nature of the event remained hidden. Adoption, after all, was sanctified by the *Primer*. Nobody's children were really their own, so what was the fuss? The changeover from children as property of God to children as property of the state was easy to make.

Then we come to Horatio Alger, Alger reached the status of cosmic adviser to American institutions, press and public alike, with all those titles of his which really had only one message. That message became known by its author's name; every poor life could be "a Horatio Alger story" if it was marked by self-reliance, hard work, cheerfulness, and opportunism. *Ragged Dick, The Luck of a Plucky Boy,* all of them — they were all the same story. In the last quarter of the century his publisher moved a million copies of the titles a year, and there were many, many bootleg copies about to swell the total.

What isn't well-known is that Alger was an ordained Unitarian minister who had left his congregation near Boston rather than answer questions about his relationships with young boys. In 1866 he became associated with the management of the Newsboy's Lodging House, a home for foundlings and runaway boys. The structure still stands at 295 East Eighth Street in New York City. In the atmosphere of the lodging house he began the career that would make him famous and create the mythic American boy hero. The effect on American culture of Alger heroes is hardly over yet. It parallels the cowboy figure, the man who settles problems with a gun. Both emblems are emblazoned on the American heart.

A fascinating coincidence lies just beneath the surface of the Alger story. It seems the very man who was the originator of the Baby Trains was also the founder of the Newsboy's Lodging Houses, and Director of the Children's Aid Society, the generating agency for the westward shipment of adopted children. That man, Charles Loring Brace, once confided in his father that he was consumed by ambition and thought of little else but fame. Brace's father was founder/publisher of *The Hartford Courant* and scion of a noble Puritan family who could trace its roots to the *Arbella's* time back at the beginning of things. Brace was engaged in packaging the largest bulk process adoption scheme in human history at precisely the moment he accepted Alger into his circle of hospitality.

Alger reciprocated in a dramatic way. At the heart of every story he placed the lesson that economic mobility requires geographic mobility. The ties with home had to be cut. Lucky boys had these ties cut cleanly by death, child-abuse could be seen as a blessing in disguise since it precipitated flight. An adventuresome, aggressive spirit, a positive attitude, hard work, and perseverance — these are more important things than family ties. Love is never a factor in an Alger story, although generosity in giving material things is, especially once economic success has been achieved. It is a message consistent with the sermons of Boston Unitarian philosophy.

The Newsboy's Lodging House which inspired Alger provided Brace with approximately 300 passengers for his adoption trains each year. Brace was delighted to boast how cheap the bill to the state was. Newsboys even paid twenty-five percent of their own upkeep and, of course, those subsequently adopted were maintained at no cost at all after that.

Alger's fiction provided a method, a rationale, and a goal for American family policy toward the poor. A childless man himself, his lifelong imaginative investment in poor boys produced a body of fiction so congenial to the Anglo-Norman imagination and habit it must, perforce, be seen as "true." So many threads of American life are tied in one way or another to Alger he might fairly be joined to Brace, Horace Mann, Fanny Wright, John Stuart Mill, and a small handful of others as a principal builder of family life in the New World.

American literary historian Van Wyck Brooks called him "this strange creature" in one of his books and surely Horatio Alger was that. His diary refers to frequent sexual expeditions to Chinatown in search of furtive venereal thrills when he tired of inspiring boys. Brooks adds:

> "Alger wrote for city boys whose only motive was self-advancement and whose "excellence" was hypocrisy and humbug. In adapting Yankee morality to a motive essentially vulgar, he made the morality itself a reproach and byword."

The theory of state intervention into family affairs that allowed mass-adoption as one of its tools was sustained and encouraged by Horatio Alger and *The New England Primer*; in a sense both made a living off the principles of adoption. This has been kept well-hidden by a crust of romantic rhetoric since the start of the twentieth century. A useful insight into what adoption really is as a political tool can be had by seeing it as one branch on the tree of eugenic mating, an idea first developed in the *Republic* and elaborated scientifically in Johann Andrea's *Christianopolis* (1619) and Tommasso Campanella's *City of the Sun* (1623). Not many people, of course, read these books, but the few who did were indeed in a choice position to act upon them, and to preempt their logic as the basis for a new political hermeticism of the powerful.

Campanella's *Magistrate for Love* sees that all citizens mate and reproduce according to eugenic principles. These titles along with Thomas More's *Utopia*, Hobbes' *Leviathan*, Bacon's *New Atlantis*, Harrington's *Oceana*, a handful of Milton's political tracts, and some few others worked their vision securely into every reform organization for centuries. They proved conclusively the truth hidden inside all apparently passive/reactive judicial systems — that the power to interpret is the power to define. To make such a real family policy work when defined in this way is more difficult, naturally. Something is needed to sway public opinion in favor of radical moves such as adoption.

And before the machinery of fulfillment came into play a course had to be charted first, a route such as would serve as a guide from the Massachusetts' Bay Colony, all of whose first governors over a span of 125 years came from two tiny villages in the south of England — Boston or New York — to Horatio Alger's country. Only a race of seafarers could have put such blind faith in a blueprint, only a race of adventurers who had left their own families behind and were forced to trust abstract maps. In the laboratories of Calvinistic America such a map was fashioned, one that would enable the mariner to hold a true course even in the most unexpected weathers and even if the crew went insane.

It was a grand design, a chart over which a pilgrim could plot his progress until he finally arrived over at the President's mansion in Oyster Bay, Long Island, where in 1912 publisher Frank Munsey told Teddy Roosevelt in the presence of several distinguished witnesses that the time had come for the state to step out of the shadows and take over the management of the American family. And so it did. All of our families are heirs to the result. Look around you.

A Different Kind of Teacher

Last week I picked up the *Poughkeepsie Journal* in a luncheon-ette near Vassar. Over coffee I started to read a piece by an actor entitled *The Actor's Mind*. Fine, I thought, tell me something about acting. But here is how the thing opened: "As a young man in high school facing my future I only knew one career I didn't want. And that was a schoolteacher's."

Ouch! After thirty years as a teacher, you might think I had become accustomed to such characterizations. To the population at large I'm afraid teachers are regarded as people to be patron-ized. What makes this disrespect doubly chilling is that teaching is the most watched line of work in the world. Nearly everybody has observed what we do because nearly everybody was locked up with us from childhood until early adulthood. We can't claim the rea-son people think badly of us is because they don't know what we are about. They know all too well.

It's not only those outside the profession who express an en-during dissatisfaction with teaching, but insiders as well. Year after year we witness a large turnover among those teachers lucky enough to have career options. In the wealthy Manhattan school district where I taught for many years, teachers come and go like leaves in autumn. And in nearly all schools the most desirable "teaching" jobs are those involving little or no contact with children.

Why is this? Perhaps because those who remain in teaching for any considerable time, barring a few saboteurs and loonies, can never be more than the instruments of policy made in remote chambers by unknown men and women. Even in alternative schools, in every matter concerning public policy, teachers are willing agents for others — or they are fired.

Many things conspire to conceal this reality. At the head of the list is the curious teacher certification process that favors young, tractable acolytes fresh out of college and licenses them for long-term, seminary-like confinement in schools, away from the world and each other. It is a weird, quasi-monastic, lifetime commitment for those who stay.

Another factor is the extremely shallow nature of intellectual enterprise in schools. Ideas are broken into fragments called subjects, subjects into units, units into sequences, sequences into lessons, lessons into homework, and all these prefabricated pieces make a classroom teacherproof. The lack of intellectual ambition forced on schoolteachers and students alike produces in them a smallness of personal presence, which is further diminished by a cacophony of ringing bells and announcements, and by endless interruptions for testing, counseling, and special events.

Most teachers don't treat themselves or their work seriously enough to run afoul of the people who make policy. Science teachers, for instance, teach the way they are told, though to do so is the antithesis of what science means. These teachers sell ritual procedures and memorization as science to kids who will never know any better. A different kind of teacher would help kids design original experiments, test hypotheses, and search for truth. Imagine millions of children unleashed to follow the road to discovery in uniquely personal ways. Of course, any teacher who really did that would be fired.

It might help you to see my point if we compare teachers and surgeons. If a respected surgeon explained to you that your kidney had to be removed, no barrier other than your own agreement would stand in the way. This would be true even if another less convincing surgeon energetically advised you to keep both kidneys in place.

In contrast, if a schoolteacher prescribed three days of independent study and only two days of class per week for a particular student, and assuming both student and family agreed, who could allow it? The principal? The district superintendent? The local school board? The state education department? The teachers' union? The Dean of a teachers' college? A court? The federal Department of Education? None of these agencies has the absolute power to release an individual from the lock-step march; each could be battered by political opposition. Only an act of the state legislature, which would require years of lobbying, could do it. A surgeon may tinker with a kidney much more easily than a teacher may tinker with schooling laws.

Schoolteachers aren't allowed to do what they think best for each student. Harnessed to a collectivized regimen, they soon give up thinking seriously about students as one-of-a-kind individuals, regardless of what they may wish were true. The two-faced aspect of schoolteaching — in which teachers are forced to act as principals when they are merely agents, forced to pretend that insignificant work has important connections with human development — is the major reason teaching is held in such low regard.

If our present, weary school-reform hysteria is not to end where all the others have ended — in more of the same — we must bell the cat of school restructuring. Alterations in time, place, and text are not enough. We won't get different schools from the same kind of teacher any more than we'll get a different piece of cake from the same old recipe. Schoolteachers will corrupt new structures just by being themselves. And whatever is wrong with teachers, it's clear that colleges and teacher certification procedures have been unable to fix it. We need to accept that there exists no scientific formula by which a good teacher can be "trained" as if he or she were a circus dog. We need to reinvent the teacher.

Teachers teach who they are. If they are incomplete people, they reproduce their incompleteness in their students. Institutions like our teacher certification process prevent people from becoming whole by imposing machine logic and directives on human life.

The American system of teacher training was inspired by nineteenth-century Prussian philosophers, who introduced compulsory schooling to the world and encouraged the creation of a teacher proletariat that would serve the state as efficiently as an army. Prussian teachers were allowed to teach nothing personal or substantive; they were trained like soldiers to take orders from staff experts. American educators, enamored of German philosophy, eagerly adopted the Prussian plan with some cosmetic differences, mostly rhetorical. Our teachers have been trained this way for more than a century, and the deadening effect on individual thinking is the same. This kind of teacher training locks the mind into an official straitjacket. It arrests development instead of enhancing it. It prevents men and women from becoming competent adults.

Our current form of state schooling, like the military, requires people who unthinkingly obey orders. Such are our teachers —

people who do as they are told. A few of these docile and compliant people are elevated to positions of small authority as school administrators, but they are still beholden to powerful people behind the scenes for their good job.

Earlier this century, American schools were further burdened by the oppressive influence of Andrew Carnegie, John D. Rockefeller, J. P. Morgan, and a small handful of other robber barons. Their determination to build an efficient industrial state led them to articulate a plan to systematize the rearing of the young. At the core of this social strategy was the removal of important decisions from familial and individual control and their reassignment to a legion of specialists. The Carnegie Foundation dubbed this system "welfare capitalism." It offered traditional libertarian freedoms to the executive and entrepreneurial classes and forced a form of state socialism on the rest of us. What we lost in freedom, it was argued, we would gain in security.

One by-product of this rethinking of government was the wholesale breaking of human bonds to other people and particular places. We were all made homeless by it. I think it was a bad bargain. Without personal command over time and without the rights to associate freely with others and to speak freely, life begins to lose its meaning. You can still walk around, but you are dying.

The most striking evidence that we are drowning in a sea of meaninglessness is our growing prison population. Currently we are incarcerating 1.2 million men and women, and 2.8 million more are either paroled convicts or ex-cons — one in every sixty-five citizens. Ours is a system proceeding toward meltdown. The crisis in our schools is not one of reading and writing but of meaning. Until we can decontrol our economy and localize it into thousands of independent communities; until we can decontrol our social system and localize it in the lives of individuals and families; and until we can see the truth that important life choices are not the proper province of any professional establishment, the meaninglessness will continue to grow.

Lecturing age-grouped children in cellblock rooms of featureless buildings is a nightmarish way to teach. (And please don't bring to mind images of slum schools; I'm thinking of wealthy, suburban schools.) What it does to teachers — not to mention students — isn't pleasant to see. It's not a matter of intelligence or goodwill. If a person enters the teaching profession with no mature skills, no powerful family ties, no deeply rooted personal culture, no traditions, no sense of God, no familiarity with real work, and no independent nature, it will be impossible to acquire them on the job.

I assume a natural urge exists in all of us to become complete, an urge frustrated by squandering too much time obeying the urgencies of other people. This is as true for teachers as it is for students. If we were candid, we'd admit that a prominent characteristic among the millions who teach school is that they are incomplete. Here's why: the center of any real person can never be the urgency of an official body. Whole people resist being told what to do and so are natural enemies of schooling. Schools know this. Hence schools socialize teachers to destroy their wholeness. Constant confinement with unhappy children, sterile workplaces, dependence on routines, low-grade intellectual material, lack of privacy, relentless isolation from colleagues, exclusion from policy making — all these stigmas of inferior status quickly wear down teachers, or drive them into administration. By teaching who they are, such people inadvertently do harm.

I know there must be teachers and schools you think are exceptions to this indictment, perhaps your own, but I have to disagree. No school agency is strong enough to guarantee the integrity of the sanctuary of which you're thinking. Of course, there are places where teachers are given some freedom because of the personal philosophy of the principal or the character of the community. But when fundamental rights depend on someone's whim, you really have no rights, only privileges that may be withdrawn at any minute. The illusion is sustained only by ignoring the real price paid in deference and dishonesty. We could take a cue from Mary Foley, a homeschooling mother of four children in Cape Cod, who was recently taken to court by the local school superintendent for refusing to report what she is teaching at home. In a statement to the court she said:

> If we are not free to educate our children, our liberty is an illusion. I do not have a curriculum. I have never used one. . . . The state does not have the power to standardize children. My education philosophy precludes the use of a curriculum. My method has been successful enough to produce a daughter who is a member of the National Honor Society and twin sons who . . . tested in the top one percent on a national placement test for two consecutive years. The priorities of our curriculum are daydreaming, natural and social sciences, self-discipline, respect of self and others, and making mistakes.

Foley is the kind of schoolteacher that we should be trying to form, one who seeks out the secret of teaching the way a child learns and who finds the courage to do so in spite of what the government directs. I wouldn't want my own children with any other kind of teacher.

You teach who you are. You teach who you are and were as a son or daughter. That's an important part of completing your own humanity and a necessary link with the world's most fundamental institution, the family. You teach who you are as a parent and as a relation. If you aren't these things you teach why not, and what you've made of yourself instead. Even if never a word is said about it you teach these things loud and clear. Teaching who you are leads toward wholeness — in yourself as well as your student. And if we don't strain toward wholeness, what is the point of teaching at all besides a paycheck?

All that I worked for throughout my thirty-year teaching career was to make myself whole. I can't say I totally succeeded, but I never stopped trying. That helps to explain my otherwise shocking confession that nothing I did in the classroom wasn't directly useful to me. I approached my teaching on a daily basis with the question, "What's in this for me?" The fallout from my struggles to become whole was the only thing I had to give my students.

The kids I had the most profound effect upon as a teacher were invariably those who were incomplete in the same ways I had been at their age, and those who lacked certain strengths I myself was struggling to learn as an adult. I taught these kids best because I was really teaching myself. Our mutual attempts to solve character problems were the field on which we wrote some notable academic successes.

I am suggesting from my experience that much of the prepared curricula, officially approved materials, formal spaces, testing, various specialized licenses, and the rest of the usual school rigmarole is wasteful and irrelevant. Teaching is some kind of connection between people, not rules on a piece of paper. It's a continuous demonstration, not tricks of information processing. This is why great parents are the greatest teachers of all. Parents don't communicate with their offspring through drills, blackboard notes, or worksheets, but through dynamic illustrations of who they are and what is important to them.

In order to reinvent the teacher, we must ask ourselves, "Who would make the best teachers of our teachers?" One resource we've overlooked is old people, who have had years to reflect on who they've been and what they've seen. Here is noble work and real status for millions of the aged. And who better could call attention to what really matters? They could use their own lives to illustrate where teaching hit the mark and where it missed, what they could have been taught that now, at the end, they realize was missing from their education.

Another untapped resource for educating teachers lies in the failed schoolteachers who are struggling to understand their failure. In my own teaching career, I learned nothing from graduate school and little from good teachers, but I got a world of insight from disappointed teachers, some of whom became my close friends. They spoke to me, and they will speak to you if they think you care to hear. They will tell you who they might have been and why they were not.

But the single most magnificent resource we've neglected in training our teachers is the huge number of children oppressed by schooling. We ignore them, I think, because we dare not look them in the eye and acknowledge their right to rage at the torment we are inflicting upon them. Instead of excluding them, we should invite them to participate in teacher formation. At last year's Spokane homeschool convention, six hundred of the fifteen hundred attendees were children, of all ages, who fully entered into all the proceedings. Their energy was dazzling and proper, as it might always be, under the guidance of whole teachers.

It's time to discard the people who hold the business of schooling tight against their chests, time to discount the advice of those who make a good living out of the current system, time to jettison the true believers. Only those dedicated to the struggle for personal, not collective, sovereignty can realistically begin to talk about a different kind of schoolteacher, one who can deliver to children a statement of his or her own aggressive independence. Without that, school reform is a waste of time.

Part Three
The Search for Meaning

In Defense of Original Sin: The Neglected Genius of American Spirituality

I was recently invited to speak at the Naropa Institute in Boulder, Colorado, as part of a conference on spirituality in education. On a warm evening in June, I found myself sitting on a camp chair under a big white tent directly in front of Tenzin Gyatso, the fourteenth Dalai Lama. He was on a stage about a dozen feet away, and there was nobody between us. As he spoke, our eyes met now and then, and I listened with growing delight as he talked about Buddhist views on wisdom and the world. Much of what he said was familiar to me: that love and compassion are human necessities; that forgiveness is essential; that Western education lacks a dimension of heart; that Americans need to rely more on inner resources. But some of his presentation was surprising. At one point, he told this audience of Americans — many of them there to increase their understanding of Buddhism — that it is better to stick with the wisdom traditions of one's own land than to run from them, pursuing in exotic locales what was under one's nose all the time.

It doesn't take a wise person to see that Americans have been substantially separated from their own wisdom tradition by forces opposed to its continuance. No mechanism has been more effective in accomplishing this than the public school system. The amazing insights of American Christian spirituality — and Protestant dissent in particular — have been relentlessly suppressed over the past century by a new global orthodoxy using compulsory schooling as its laboratory and training around. And no, I am not a Protestant. You don't have to be a Protestant to recognize that the abandonment of our homegrown wisdom tradition by policymaking elites has left our educational system spiritually bereft.

Although the American Christian tradition draws on European and Near Eastern roots, and has been fertilized by a variety of faiths throughout its course, the particular genius of American Christianity is primarily derived from the Protestant reformation in Britain — a movement not only opposed to the official, systematic state church, but also, in a fundamental sense, a protest against *system itself.* This independent and dissenting religious tradition shifted responsibility for salvation from the political system to the individual.

In early America, Protestant dissent came in many different forms: Congregational, Presbyterian, Anabaptist, Quaker, and so on. From these independent interpretations of the Hebrew Bible and the stories of a long-dead Jewish carpenter came the basis for the Declaration of Independence, the Constitution, and the Bill of Rights, documents virtually without precedent in history. The Bill of Rights alone conferred powers on ordinary citizens — such as the right of free assembly, the right to free speech, the right to own weapons, and the right to deny the state access to one's home — that were (and are) unique on the planet. Out of these rights, derived both by accident and by design from the American Christian tradition of dissent, came the curriculum of early schooling in this country up until the Civil War.

Whatever its surface variations, this curriculum was intended to preserve the hard-won rights thought necessary to the life of an independent, dissenting Christian. It produced, for example, the American tradition of common argument — not the kind that leads to a dueling scar among the elites of Brandenberg, but the kind that leads to a broken nose in a beer hall in Pittsburgh, or to a magnificent statesman like William Jennings Bryan throwing away his political career in defense of small farmers. The American tradition of argument — our God-given right to damn the king, whoever that king may be — is a precious legacy handed down to us by British Protestants, not the Church of England, nor any secular tradition, either.

When English Puritans reached Salem in 1629, there were no Anglican officials present to certify their choice of leaders, so they took that responsibility — illegally — into their own hands. That simple, yet revolutionary, act transferred enormous political power to ordinary churchgoers, whose sole qualification to wield such power was that they had joined a congregation that took religion seriously. Historians dubbed this quiet insurrection the Salem Procedure, and for the next 231 years this shedding of traditional authority — an act of monumental localism — challenged the right of arrogant rulers to disseminate their version of the truth without its facing review by the American people. This became the only nation in history where ordinary citizens could take issue with authority without being beaten, jailed, or killed.

Congregations were never universal in focus, but always intensely local. Members knew their fellow congregants by name and family history. These were not mere networks of people who met in church on Sunday if it was convenient. The congregants cared about each other in particular more than about humanity in general. And if a congregation had a problem, it would not accept outside intervention unless all other possibilities had been exhausted. These groups insisted upon doing things their own way and making their own mistakes.

Were some of these congregations bad? Sure, some of them were horrible. But at least the damage stopped at the boundaries of a single church and community. That's the difference between a Congregational model and a state-church system, or indeed any systematic form of universal governance: a system won't let you walk away, whereas a congregation will say, "Good-bye and good riddance."

We are far from a time when we trusted ourselves to run our own lives without surveillance. Since the Civil War, nearly a century and a half of increasingly suffocating "expert" intervention in our schools and elsewhere has left us thinking that, to decide anything important, we have to call in Harvard, or Stanford, or Yale, or the Carnegie Corporation — all honorable institutions, but also outsiders, strangers. As a consequence, our children have no goal to aim for apart from the approval of these official strangers. I suspect such expert interventions are one reason why families are falling apart. How can children respect their parents when those sad souls are regularly contradicted by various representatives of the state? Parents have been made childlike by this "Expert Procedure," just as the Puritans were given full adulthood by the Salem Procedure.

The Salem Procedure is completely antagonistic to the current model because it consists in lay people picking their own experts and keeping them on a very short tether. It also draws from the well of common-sense wisdom found among people who actually work, rather than talk, for a living — small farmers, craftspeople, teamsters, artists, fishermen, loggers, small entrepreneurs, laborers, housemaids, and so on. I say wisdom because, of course, experts are expected to have superior knowledge. But to conflate the two, as our century has done, is madness. Going to college can help you become knowledgeable — an "expert," even — but it cannot make you wise, not even a little bit. Wisdom cannot be so easily purchased. The American genius was to locate wisdom in ordinary people, whereas every other government on earth located it in an aristocracy, theocracy, military class, merchant class, or counterfeit meritocracy.

The Congregational principle is a spiritual force that encourages the greatest number of people to reach their full potential by vesting everyone with responsibility, identity, and a voice — and this is accomplished in voluntary associations of members who are in harmony with one another. That's the way the Council on Foreign Relations works, and the Advertising Council, and the Business Round Table. It's the way Sidwell Friends School works, and St. Paul's, and Groton. And it's the way public schools would work best, too. (Think about this obvious discrepancy for a while, and you'll begin to wonder what purpose is served by structuring government schools any other way.) The congregationalists knew that good things happen to the human spirit when it is left alone to make its own curriculum. The descendants of some of those congregationalists now run the country, and have remembered this lesson for their own children. But they have failed to remember that the American experiment demands equality for all.

Significantly, no two Congregational churches ever got together, even to compare notes. Neither did they inquire after each other's doctrinal purity. They maintained no centralized management, and often discharged ministers who got too big for their britches. Some were good, some horrible, but each was sovereign.

No doctrine of Christianity has been more controversial, or more central to Christian vocation, than the doctrine of original sin. At its starkest, original sin is the frightening moral principle that the sins of the parents are visited upon the children. In the intense three-way religious debates that marked life in early America, settlers from the core of the Protestant Reformation tradition upheld the doctrine of original sin, defending it against attacks by liberal Christian groups like the Unitarians and Universalists, who vehemently rejected the notion that a grave, inescapable verdict had been handed down on all of us, and against attacks by the newly minted corporate mind, obsessed with order, regulation, and profit, rather than salvation. The extermination of the doctrine of original sin sat at the top of both the liberal and the corporate agendas. The former group found it an intolerable obstacle to the pursuit of happiness, and the latter, to the pursuit of profit.

Thus, when a legislative mandate made school attendance compulsory, an unwritten mandate was also passed on to schoolteachers to rid the modern world of the doctrine of original sin, which had occupied such a central position in the organization of American life. It was nearly a century before that policy was put in writing, when the 1947 Supreme Court decision in the Everson case established that the state would have no truck with religion. Schooling was to be about the creation of loyalty to a principle of abstract central authority, and no serious rival — whether parents, tribe, tradition, self, or God — would be welcome in school. Corporate economics and the developing modern culture eliminated the other rivals, but it took the highest court in the land to bar God. It's obvious from this decision that the state considers American religious tradition to be dangerous. And of course it is.

Before Everson, 150 years had passed without any court finding this fantastic hidden meaning in the Constitution. But we can forgo examining the motives of the Everson court, and even concede that the ruling is a sincere expression of the rationale behind modern leadership, without waiving our right to challenge the law's legitimacy on the grounds of the grotesque record of the past fifty years. Spiritless schooling has been thoroughly tested and found wanting — in my opinion because it denies metaphysical realities recognized by men and women worldwide, in every age.

As valuable a tool as rational thought is, it doesn't speak to the depths of human nature — our feelings of loneliness and incompleteness, our sense of sin, our need to love, and our longing for immortality. To illustrate how rational thinking alone makes a wretched mess of human affairs, I will mount an attack on the scientific model of the universe.

As Galileo famously showed, the sun — not the earth — is at the center of the solar system. And we all know that the solar system itself is only a puny thing lost in endless space. And yet to date it looks as if only Earth can support human life. I know Carl Sagan said we'll find millions of populated planets eventually, but right now there's hard evidence of only one. We can't live anyplace but Earth for long. So, as of today, Earth is, for all intents and purposes, the center of the human universe.

To push this line of reasoning a little further, where your life is concerned, Earth is most certainly not the center, but merely a background that floats in and out of conscious thought. You are the center of your universe, because if you don't show up, it doesn't exist. This may sound self-absorbed, but the minute you deny your own centrality, you betray the rest of us. You are then fleeing your responsibility — as the most important person in the universe — to make things better. When you deny your centrality, you lose trust in yourself. (And school is there to drill you in distrusting yourself.) As that trust wanes, you lose self-respect, without which you can't like yourself very much. How can you like someone you don't respect or trust?

And it gets worse, for when you don't like yourself very much you lose the ability to sustain loving relationships with others. Think of it this way: you must first be convinced of your own worth before you ask for someone else's love, or else the bargain will be unsound. You'll be passing off low-grade merchandise — yourself — as the real McCoy.

The trouble with science is that its truths are only partial. Galileo had the facts right about the dead matter of the solar system, but said nothing about the cosmology of the human spirit. Yet schools can teach only Galileo's victory over the Church, not his spiritual error. Galileo's observations are only a microscopic part of a real education; his blindness is much more to the point. The primary goal of real education is not to deliver facts but to guide students to the truths that will allow them to take responsibility for their lives. In that quest, Galileo is no help at all.

The neglected genius of American spirituality is that it grants dignity and responsibility to ordinary individuals, not to elites. This tradition, grounded in the doctrine of original sin, paradoxically identifies the core problems of living as the fundamental bases for inner peace and happiness. Rather than suggesting strategies to combat or flee these problems, American Christianity demanded they be accepted willingly as conditions of human life in a fallen world.

Whether or not we accept the biblical story of Adam and Eve at face value, we are all stuck with the burdens that Christianity ascribes to original sin. Nobody can escape — regardless of wealth, intellect, charm, powerful connections, or scientific miracles. Whether we are good or bad cuts no mustard. Everyone is in for it.

The Christian reading of Genesis identified four specific penalties that attended expulsion from Eden. First, there was the penalty of work: there had been no work in Eden, but now we would have to provide for ourselves. Second, there was the penalty of pain: there had been no pain in Eden, but now we would be subject to tremendous suffering, even from such natural acts as childbirth. Third, there was the penalty of free will: in Eden there had been exactly one wrong thing to do, but now we would have to be morally wary, because every decision would be good or evil or a million shades in between. And last was the penalty of death: in Eden we might have lived forever, but now the term of human life would be strictly limited, and the more wealth, health, beauty, family, community, and friends we had, the more we would be tempted at the end of life to curse God as we witnessed ourselves losing it all, day by day.

That's some doom, I'm sure you'll agree. The question is what to do about it. Historically, two different answers emerged. Some folks cast in their lot with shrewdness, calculation, and science to find a way out, and that group has commanded our schools, our economy, our technology, and our public life for over a century. Here is its response to the penalties of original sin:

On work: Work is a necessary evil for the masses, but an avoidable inconvenience for the smart ones. Machines and electronic devices are making most work obsolete. Only stupid people work; the enlightened can make a living exploiting and regulating others, paying them to mine the rock and harvest the earth.

On pain: Science provides ways to avoid pain and enhance pleasure. Chemicals and modern medicine will eventually render pain unnecessary. Feeling good is what life's all about; there isn't anything else.

On good and evil: There is no absolute good or evil. Every principle is negotiable, all ethics are situational, and right and wrong are relative. Don't worry about God's punishment. With enough knowledge, we can duplicate the power of the mythical God. So God destroyed Sodom and Gomorrah with fire; we turned the night sky over the desert to flame and incinerated a hundred thousand retreating Iraqis in a matter of seconds. We are God.

On aging and death: Science can stave off sickness and extend life. Aging must be concealed as long as possible through surgery, dress, personal-training regimens, and attitude make-overs. Survival is the highest goal, so it follows that the health industry wields the ultimate power. Every day, science gets closer and closer to making life eternal.

You see how easy it is to repudiate the penalties of original sin? From the start, this has been one of the main missions of forced schooling: to direct people's loyalty away from the organizing principles of a religious life and reattach it to the values of corporate industry, government, and professionals. Only the secular establishment would grant absolution.

What American spirituality taught was much different. It advised us to embrace punishment rather than avoid it, and taught the marvelous paradox that willing acceptance of our human burdens is the only way to a good, full life. If you bend your head in obedience, it will be raised up strong, brave, indomitable, and wise. Look at the difference, step by step:

On work: Work is the only avenue to genuine self-respect. Work develops independence, self-reliance, resourcefulness, and character. Without real work we will inevitably find despair, no matter how much money or power we have. Work has value far beyond a paycheck, praise, or accomplishment, and produces spiritual rewards unrelated to the reinforcement schedules of behavioral psychologists, but only if we tackle it gladly, without resentment.

By teaching the secular aversion to work, schools have created a horrifying problem that has so far proven incurable — the spiritual anxiety that arises when we have no useful work. Phony work, no matter how well paid or highly praised, results in emotional disturbance. Major efforts have gone into solving this problem, but there's no hint of an answer in sight. In our economy, the real dilemma now is keeping people occupied. Jobs have to be invented by government agencies and corporations, both of which employ millions of people for whom they have no real use. Young men and women at their brightest, orneriest, and most energetic are kept from working because they would either work too eagerly or invent their own jobs, which could cause a cataclysm in the economy. We cannot afford to let children learn to work for fear they will discover one of the great secrets of history: work is not a curse but a salvation.

On pain: Pain is a friend, because it forces our attention away from the world and refocuses it squarely back on ourselves. Pain of all sorts is the way we learn insight, balance, and self-control. The siren call of "Feel good!" lures us to court desirable sensations and to despise pain as a spoiler of pleasure. Pain, however, is the road to self-knowledge.

On good and evil: In a spiritual life everything is morally charged; nothing is neutral. Choosing between good and evil is a daily effort, but taking responsibility for your choices makes you fully alive. I recently heard about a woman who was having an affair openly in front of her husband and her six-year-old daughter. "It's no big deal," the woman told her mother. But if infidelity and the shattering of a child's innocence are no big deal, then what is? When we intensify our moral awareness, everything becomes a big deal.

To enhance life we must stop making preprogrammed choices. The fewer choices we make automatically, as if we were only machines, the bigger our lives will become, because every choice will have a moral dimension. Despite any excuses we may make — and there are legions of fine ones — the record of our choices marks us as worthy or unworthy. Even if nobody else knows what rats we are, deep inside us the running balance of our accounts will vitally affect our ability to trust, to love, and to gain peace and wisdom.

On aging and death: This world is only a stage in some longer journey we do not understand. To fall in love with our physical beauty, wealth, health, or capacity for pleasure is to kid ourselves, because all that will be taken away. Upon the death of her husband of sixty years (who had left her millions of dollars) my aunt said to me tearfully, "They don't let you win! There is no way to win!" She had lived her life in the camp of science, honorably observing all its rules of rationality. But at this final pass science was a useless ally. The Christian tradition would say that you can win — and if you think you can't, then you're playing the wrong game.

The only thing that gives our choices any deep significance is the fact that none of this will last. Awareness of mortality gives relationships an urgency, makes our choices matter. If we were immortal, how could it possibly mean a hill of beans whether we did something today, tomorrow, or next year? There would always be more time later, so we wouldn't have to live now.

Everyone has experienced having too much of something — candy, sex, company. We can even have too much money, such that no individual purchase involves real choice, because real choices always close the door on other choices: if you can buy everything, why bother to buy anything? For the same reason, it's possible to have too much time: if there's time for everything, why bother to do anything at all? The solution is full awareness that time is preciously finite. You have less now than when you started reading this, so hurry; the clock is ticking! As you spend time on one thing, you lose the chance forever to spend it on something else. Science cannot help you one bit with time. Indeed, using scientific methods to save time is the best way to guarantee your life will be eaten alive by trivial matters, none of which will ever be any big deal.

The best lives seem to be full of contemplation, solitude, and self-examination; full of private, personal attempts to engage the riddles of existence, from the cosmic mystery of death to the smaller mystery of exchanging secrets with a cat. When I see kids day-dreaming in school, I am careful never to shock them out of their reverie. What I have to say can wait. We make the most of our limited time by alternating hard effort with still moments free of the cultural imperative to "get something." If such solitude seems impossible in the world we live in, consider that, in spite of all the hype about global communication, sixty-seven percent of the world's population has never made or received a single phone call.

I may seem to have strayed from the topic of American spirituality, but I haven't, really. Until we understand that the factual contents of our minds — the "truths" upon which we base our decisions — have for the most part been inserted there by others whose motives are not our own, we will never fully appreciate the unique gift of American Christian spirituality. For it teaches that the answers to our problems lie within us, that we are the center of the universe, and that wisdom cannot be learned in school, but only through accepting the burden of work, learning the lessons pain teaches, sorting out right and wrong for ourselves, and coming to terms with aging and death. If these are our spiritual compasses, we need no rulers or experts to tell us how to live.

American spirituality offers a set of practical guidelines, street lamps for the village of our lives. Although the focus is on the individual, nobody is asked to wander aimlessly. What constitutes a good life is clearly spelled out: self-knowledge, duty, responsibility, compassion, acceptance of loss, preparation for death. In this neglected tradition, no teacher does your work. You must do it for yourself.

Beyond Money: The Purpose of Learning (and Life)

My mother takes in stray animals, mostly homeless dogs and cats, but if a hurt bird's wing needs repair, birds also. If a turtle is crossing the road too slowly, she makes my father stop the car so she can get out and carry it to the other side of the road. When Dad objected to how many animals our household was supporting, mother took to setting large dishes of Nabisco dog food in our back yard for the wanderers, an act of generosity that made our house look like a kennel and drove my father frantic, not least because he was the manager of the local National Biscuit Company.

The other day I was reading *Proverbs,* a collection of advice set down by Solomon 3,000 years ago, when I came across these words:

"Speak up for those who cannot speak for themselves." Speak up for those who cannot speak for themselves? Suddenly I realized what my mother had done all those years I thought she was just feeding animals. She was speaking for those who couldn't speak for themselves. And reading further into *Proverbs* I found this:

"Happy are they who are generous to the poor." Happy are they who are generous to the poor? Reading those words I realized I had part of the secret that made my mother happy, for she was happy most of the time I was growing up in spite of a full share of her own troubles. She was unfailingly generous to the poor — not just to outcast creatures, but to anyone who came to our door for a handout, to any neighborhood person fallen on hard times and needing help. I had a little lawn-mowing business in those days, and I remember in particular the widow with young children whose lawn I mowed for free because my mother asked me to.

I suppose I read *Proverbs* the way most people do who pick up a Gideon Bible in a motel room. I jump about not looking for anything in particular. So it was while randomly turning the pages I found this judgment, and by implication this warning, too:

"There is joy for those who seek the common good." Joy for those who seek the common good. And I remembered my mother's beautiful Christmas trees that took days of hard effort to create, effort in the family's common service. I remembered her collecting of kitchen grease and metal scrap for the war effort in the long gone days of World War II, and her fierce defense of equity as head of the PTA, and her founding a Cub Scout Troop when none of the local men could be persuaded to do it. I remembered the joy she brought to so many undertakings of my boyhood.

The Economist announced recently that seventy percent of all the lawyers in the world are in the United States. We have twenty-five times the number of lawyers per capita that Japan does, three and a half times the number that England has, two and a half times the number per capita in Germany. If you add our public and private practice lawyers together, about one in every 250 Americans is a lawyer.

What could the meaning of this be? Seventy percent of all the world's lawyers? Before he died, Joseph Campbell took note of our enormous legal fraternity and called it the way Americans talk to each other, the way employees talk to bosses and brothers to sisters. Lawsuits are the way we get the other guy's attention because we have lost the normal interest in each other, lost the concern for human face-to-face justice, lost the taste for plain speaking that marks a healthy people.

Looking at the great tradition of English common law, there are only two reasons to bring a case at all: first, that someone hasn't kept a promise, has not done what they said they would do. That gives rise to contract law. And second, that someone has encroached on another person's rights and done harm. That gives rise to tort and criminal law.

So if you are looking for a new way to mark the crisis in American society, if you are wary of hearing about teenage suicide, divorce, crime, violence, alienated brothers and sisters, murder, drugs, etc. even one more time, then think on the barometer of crisis represented by seventy percent of the world's lawyers collecting under the American eagle's wing. There must be a tremendous number of us breaking our promises, and a tremendous number of us encroaching on rights to support such a battalion of barristers.

We are forgetting, I think, how to live together in families and communities; forgetting the necessary personal duties that make families and communities in the first place, in a rush to get out from under personal responsibility. To escape. How often do you hear the cry, "Let them do it! They get paid for it!" When "them" can mean police or street sweepers or social workers or any of a number of other occupational titles that have come to identify our transition from a world of human beings who live together and care about each other to a world of institutions and hired hands.

What does it mean when we break our promises so often? What does it mean when we encroach so often on each other's rights? When we abandon personal responsibility for the common

good so completely to people we hire that the air is full of our re-
fusals and stony silences, all eyes rigidly turned away from duty,
all mouths full of, "No! Let them do it. They get paid for it."

What does it mean for your future and mine that a price tag
has been set on simple services that through the long history of
humanity were freely exchanged and even freely given? Like sitting with the sick, caring for the old, or even caring for one's own
children. Like mowing a poor widow's lawn.

If it means something frightening, what can we do about it?

At the turn of the twentieth century a profound social thinker
in France named George Simmel wrote a remarkable book called
The Philosophy of Money. In it, Simmel, one of the great creative
theorists of this century, said that money contained a powerful internal contradiction built into the foundations of its abstract existence: by robbing things of their innate identity and replacing that
core identity with a money identity, by making everything interchangeable with money, money often cheapened things and removed their significance! Simmel said that whenever genuine personal qualities like service were offered for money, that the pricing
of these things inevitably trivialized what had been priced. The
services tend to gradually become degraded, to lose distinction,
just exactly as if the money itself sharply reduced the value of what
was being purchased.

Even though that was written ninety-one years ago it still has
a shocking and almost crazy ring to it. But Simmel was quite serious and generations of blue ribbon readership have found enough
disturbing truth in his words to keep them available generation

after generation. Simmel continued: "Whenever genuine personal values have to be offered for money, one finds that a loosening, a loss of quality in individual life takes place." For instance in prostitution, a kind of temporary marriage for money, the monetization of sex leads to "a terrible degradation of personal value." Both prostitute and client are worse for the experience, not better. The sale of compassion, the sale of concern, even the sale of a helping hand in many instances, lead to the same destination. At some point pricing eats away the intangible quality of service and the central value of what is offered is destroyed. It's a complicated idea, but one well worth musing upon.

Now think again about the meaning of all those American lawsuits, think of all the broken promises they represent, the counterfeit "services" rendered. Is it just barely possible that the shift after World War II to what is called a "service" economy is part of the reason for our visible unhappiness as a nation? Is it just barely possible that when most of us don't accept the obligation of service to each other, performed freely, as part of the social contract, but instead assign the job to hired hands, that rather than the joy Solomon promised, the payoff might be its opposite, misery?

Well, I don't know the answer to that, but I do have an interesting bit of recent evidence in support of Simmel's theory. In 1971 the National Book Award for nonfiction went to a title called *The Gift Relationship: From Human Blood to Social Policy* by Richard M. Titmuss, et al., a book which undertook to explore whether valuable things given freely — like services rendered voluntarily — were more or less valuable than the same services as part of a commercial system.

The commodity the author took for his test was human blood.

He made an imaginative, crossnational comparison of the quality and availability of human blood in countries that charge for it, like our own, and in countries like England where it is given away. Almost all blood in the U.S. is purchased wholesale and then resold several times for several profits; almost all blood in England is donated freely and then given away.

The book's conclusions aren't the slightest bit ambiguous: where blood is sold the quality is terrible, prices sky-high, shortages common; and where blood is sold there is also frequently danger to the purchaser, even in the best of hospitals. But there is an additional, intangible cost. Where blood is bought and sold, the community loses the tradition of giving freely to neighbors and strangers, and where that tradition is lost the donors lose the joy gained from service in the common good. In other words a social and ethical corrosion ensues from the market in blood. Communities which provide their own blood needs without cost are healthy in many other ways, too. People seemed happier in such communities.

Transforming blood into the stuff of commerce is inefficient in economic terms, in supply terms, and in quality terms; the social cost is high, in addition. The U.S. blood supply, the most heavily commercialized in the world, is also the worst in the world.

The lesson of my mother, of biblical Solomon, of Simmel, and of blood, I mean to be a lesson for our schools, too. When schools consume the youth of the nation in confinement, and all the products of all their labors become paper to be thrown away, there is no joy possible in the seeking of such goods. The pricing of time through grade points establishes an irrational currency by which something precious, time, is corrupted in the service of arbitrary and nonsensical urgencies.

Experts who are the sellers of school services to the government have consistently misdiagnosed and misdefined the problem of schooling. The problem is not that children don't learn to read, write, and do arithmetic very well — those deficiencies are direct by-products of our errors of definition. The problem is that kids hardly learn at all the way schools insist on teaching.

Schools desperately need a vision of their own purpose, because the vision they promulgate now is a dishonest one. It was never factually true that young people learn to read or do arithmetic primarily by being taught these things. They are learned, but not really taught at all. Overteaching interferes with learning, although the few who survive it may well come to imagine it was by an act of teaching. Colonial America was massively literate without any systematic or compulsory schooling at all.

For many decades, an artificially induced hysteria about "basic skills" has been the masquerade used to intimidate us into abandoning children to a form of schooling that simply doesn't work. Behind this mask, valuable lessons of service to a vibrant community of real human beings have been denied the young — and all of us have been denied the reciprocities healthy adults need with children across the full spectrum of ages.

Give and take; take and give. Children desperately need the lessons volunteer service, apprenticeships, and work/study teach, but instead they are kept in holding pens with others of their own age and social class. They are priced and valued according to their ability to adjust to this unhealthy regimen, to remain passive, to take orders, to maintain a cheerful demeanor while their time is wasted. They give nothing, but are rewarded for becoming quiet parasites. This has been the formula producing extended child-ishness and the outlines of a caste system in the U.S., however well it has served the economic institution of mass-schooling. After struggling at the bars of the cage for a few years, most kids just give up and settle into the low-grade vocational activities of the school. The relentless rationalization of the educational experience to one flavor, confinement schooling, has left the modern student a pris-oner in a disenchanted world without meaning.

Our cultural dilemma here in the United States has nothing to do with children who don't read very well. It lies instead in the difficulty of finding a way to restore meaning and purpose to mod-ern life. There is no point in reading if it seems to lead nowhere. We have progressively stripped children of the primary experi-ence base they need to grow up sound and whole by pricing ab-stract study higher. The great irony has been that while we have devalued service and life experience, abstraction has followed the path Simmel predicted — it, too, matters less and less.

The dynamics of this process are subtle. To begin with, the natural sequence of learning is destroyed without experience — a sequence in which hands-on experience, "primary data" to give it an academic title, must always come first. Only after a long ap-prenticeship in rich and profound contact with the world, the home, the neighborhood, does the thin gas of abstraction mean much to most people. After almost thirty years of classroom teaching I came to see what Benjamin Franklin must have realized as a teenager: Only a few of us are fashioned in such a peculiar way as to thrive on an exclusive diet of blackboard work and workbook work and bookwork work and talkwork work of all sorts. When we fail to take into account how most children, rich or poor, really learn — by involvement, by doing, by independent risk-taking, by shouldering responsibility, by intermingling intimately into the real world of adults in all its manifestations — when we set up a laboratory universe in which all are confined with anonymous strangers, then we have created in advance a world of failing families, wrecked cities, and blasted individuals. Then we have created the *mise en scene* where a mathematical bell curve seems to describe a human condition in which only a few children have any real talent.

This is a cynical act. It is only prolonged, in the face of its deadly effects, because school factories and all the forces which service them have become an integral part of the money economy. The lie of our own unexamined premises has given us the problem children we complain of as a nation. Indifferent children, cowardly children, dishonest children, selfish children, children who disrespect parents and adults in general, who hurt each other, who trample each other's rights for worthless prizes like blue ribbons or school grades. Eventually these are children who grow up to be clients for the nation of lawyers we are becoming, children who will one day break contracts and encroach on the weak if the opportunity arises.

And why not? That is the example school sets. The logic of compulsory schooling in the middle of a democracy is a contradiction of the original national charter; it breaks the contract of the Bill of Rights, using as its justification the excuse that kids can't learn any other way, that they can't be trusted with responsibility. The truth is exactly the opposite: unless they are trusted with responsibility they cannot learn much, and under the thumb of central compulsion the lessons they do learn are bad ones. School encroaches on the right of each new life to test itself against the needs of the real world. Schools are a training ground for irresponsibility because that is nearly the only thing they are set up to teach.

Schools desperately need a vision of their own purpose. At present they are exactly what many suspect, they are government jobs for children; and the worst kind of government jobs — the make-work kind, not really jobs at all.

There is nothing, or very little, to do in school. Our elite high school texts are on the level of fifth grade readers from 160 years ago, in the time before we got compulsory schooling. And dumbing down the work isn't some sinister conspiracy, it has become more and more a necessity as generations of well-schooled children succeed themselves and become parents.

So the damage is cumulative, and it is fast becoming insupportable. Look around you at our society. We have created a whirlpool of addictions much more sophisticated than drug addictions that children and grown children use to avoid confronting themselves with their own uselessness. We are reluctant to face the truth because it acts as a mirror, revealing more than we can face about the real source of our difficulties. We have forced children to be irresponsible for twelve years. It is no wonder they dislike themselves and us, and no wonder they cannot recover. Cut a man's legs off as a boy and they will not grow back when he is a man.

With the growing public alarm over the effects of science and technology on societies all over the world, we are soon going to have a chance to rethink the basic questions of education, questions which have little to do with reading, writing, and arithmetic — but much to do with the fundamental queries of human existence:

In what curriculum is a good life found?

How shall we all live?

What shall we do with our children?

My own suspicion is that systematic, confinement schooling is doomed, that there is no way to tinker with it to make it work much better, that soon the monopoly will have to be surrendered because it doesn't work. It hurts people, and it is far too expensive. If well-schooled children are the goal, they can be turned out for a fraction of the cost of government-schooled children.

John Chubb of the Brookings Institute responded to charges that breaking the government monopoly would hurt poor children and children of color by producing figures that show private and parochial schools are better integrated than public schools — at about half the cost.

But frankly, I don't think the world can afford well-schooled children at all, whether they come from factories of government, church, or private industry. We need a different kind of man and woman to tackle the future. The kind of young people who accept the obligations of living in society joyfully. To get to this new place, we need a vision of what an education is and what a school can be; only out of a clearly spoken vision can come the mutual hope we need to find ways to get there.

Curriculum is only the Latin word for a race course, the path by which the racehorse gets to its destination. We haven't even begun to agree as a nation on a destination for education that is an honest one. Beating other countries, scoring well on tests, getting a "good" job — all these are low evasions of what the human spirit needs. All are ways to duck the truth that we have failed, thus far, to pay the price in argument, debate, agony, and love that a strong vision will cost.

Without a vision all the talk about reforming "curriculum" will lead nowhere. Unless we can convince ourselves, our children included, that the new course is worth following it will not work any better than the old one did. Why should it?

It must be something all of us can share, a destiny far beyond "winning" and money and taking more than our share of material things. For the questions will always reemerge, "To what end? Why are we doing these things?"

Messy and unpleasant as it will be for a practical people like Americans, the sequence must start with clear goals. In a democracy worth the name the goals come from the bottom up, not the other way around. It will be messy if done right because hundreds and thousands of separate agendas will be set in conflict by any attempt to change what is, and we will learn, finally, that we need multiple visions, many different curricula.

If I guess right, we don't have a choice. The present course is almost over. The whole food supply is in jeopardy, for one thing. Breeding stocks of fish along the California coast are at their lowest levels in history. Cape Cod Bay, on the other side of the continent, where once the fish were thick enough to walk across, is a dead sea in many places. The radical conclusion forces itself upon us that the oceans are dying. In Kansas a bushel of irreplaceable topsoil blows away for every bushel of corn raised by factory-farming methods, and that is true in all the wheat and corn states. The food value of chemical agriculture's harvest is already much lower than that of the natural harvests of old-fashioned farming.

If my guess is right, we need to construct a new vision of what education is, and we need new race courses on which to run at that vision. The government can't do it for us; that's been tried for 140 years in the monopoly schools, but they just get worse and worse — more the creators of our problem than the solution. If my guess is right we don't even have a choice. The old system where every child was locked away and set into nonstop, daily competition with every other child for silly prizes called grades is broken beyond repair. If it could be fixed it would have been fixed by now. Good riddance.

There is no correlation between the play money of grades and the play money we buy things with except that dishonest correlation forced on the job market by rigging it with arbitrary laws and policies. For example, you can establish by law or policy that the only people who get into medical school are the people with lofty grade point averages, but that will not guarantee that the best people become doctors. That same unpleasant reality holds true for lawyers, businessman, engineers, or schoolteachers. We have yet another warning that forcing the collective time of the American young into a contest for symbols, whether money or grades or similar prizes, is a mistaken course, and that warning is found in the proverbs of Solomon, the haunting predictions of George Simmel, the frightening reality of the American blood supply, and the curious emergence of a national horde of lawyers who demonstrate our unhappiness. We do not trust each other, we do not like each other, we do not care for each other, we are unable to keep ourselves from encroaching on each other, and we cannot keep our promises. That is a recipe for social disaster, not one for a good life.

The new vision of American education is going to have to find a currency beyond money and grades with which to pay its children to learn. My own experience after fifteen years of sponsoring service learning projects for each one of my students, rich and poor, white and black, is that a curriculum that seeks the common good will be an important part of that real currency which doesn't recede or inflate. It holds its value.

My own experience has been that every single academic question that can be asked can be asked around a base of genuine service to the community, and can ride easily around an orbit of service. My own kids always did one full day of community service a week; they generally worked alone in order to escape the culture of schoolchildren; they took on full adult responsibilities and a full adult workday even at the age of twelve or thirteen. And in almost every case they discharged their duties splendidly. Even in the first year I experimented with such a program it worked. Indeed it worked better for the selfish, spoiled, indifferent children of prosperous families than it did for the lost children of the poor and non-college bound — but the differences were small. It worked for everyone including the communities which allowed themselves to be served. It transformed people spiritually, morally, and academically, too.

In Western society over the past several thousand years we have had, at various times, great social visions: the pagan vision of Stoics like Marcus Aurelius, the aristocratic vision of Charlemagne and the Plantagenets, the Christian vision of St. Augustine, of

Origen, and of the martyrs. All these grand conceptions for which curricula were developed had a service ideal at the bedrock of their foundations, a sense that we are obligated to each other, that we need duties self-imposed if we expect to live easily with ourselves. That is the great secret we have lost sight of in schools built around a philosophy or theology of materialism, a curriculum of competition and accumulation, a curriculum of self-aggrandizement — that these directives are prescriptions for bad individuals, bad communities, bad societies, and bad consciences.

All the transforming visions we have human record of asked a question beyond money: "What do I owe?" And these visions promise that if we will only speak for those who cannot speak for themselves, if we will only be generous to the poor, if we will only seek the common good, that our lives will be filled with meaning. It worked for Solomon, it worked for my mother, it will work for the rest of us, too.

What Really Matters?

This address was given on June 7, 1992, at graduation ceremonies for Evergreen State College in Olympia Washington.

Going to the moon didn't really matter, it turned out.

I say that from the vantage point of my fifty-seven years, but also because not so long ago I watched as an official astronaut in a silver space suit tried to get the attention of an auditorium full of Harlem teenagers. He came with every tricky device and visual aid NASA could muster, and he was a handsome, well-built black man in his prime with a compelling, resonant voice. Yet the audience ignored him so comprehensively that at several places in his presentation he couldn't continue. It was rude, but I learned something important.

The kids instinctively understood, I think, that he had less control over his rocket vehicle than a bus driver. I think they understood that any experiments he performed were someone else's, even if they couldn't have put that idea into words — that his talk was part of the great non-thought of received ideas. It was irrelevant whether he understood his experiments because they weren't his, he was only an agent, not a principal, in the same way bad schoolteachers are only agents.

Kids outgrow dolls, even talking ones. It seems likely to me that these kids considered going to the moon a dumb game. I can't verify that because I didn't question them, but most didn't have fathers at all or any dignity in their lives and about half never ate off a tablecloth. What is going to the moon supposed to mean? I couldn't answer that question with any confidence if I were asked, and I had a father, once, and a tablecloth.

I never heard a student, white or black, show any interest in the space business in thirty years of schoolteaching, although it filled news pages for a long time and was a regular item on the school circuit. Except when Challenger blew up, never a flicker of curiosity and even that passed in an instant. Going to the moon didn't matter much it turned out.

A lot of things don't matter that are supposed to. One is "well-funded" schools, although saying that is thought to be irresponsible by people who don't think too clearly. Over one hundred studies have tried to show a connection between money and learning; not one has succeeded. But from 1932 to 1992 schoolmen said endlessly money would buy results and we believed that. It seemed to make sense. So we invested four times more cash in inflation-adjusted dollars in 1992 than we did in 1932, invested it in certifying strangers and having them lecture to children held fast under compulsion — yet after 12,000 hours of government schooling one out of five Americans can't read the directions on a medicine bottle.

After 12,000 hours of compulsory schooling, high school graduates have no skills to trade for income or even any skills with which to talk to each other. They can't change a flat, repair a faucet, install a light, follow directions for the use of a typewriter, make change reliably, or keep their marriages together. The situation is considerably worse than television journalism comprehends.

Here is something puzzling, though. The Shelter Institute in Bath, Maine, teaches you how to build a beautiful post and beam home in three weeks — even if you're a teenager — and in another three weeks or so will teach you how to install a sewer system, water, heat, and electric. Owning a home is the foremost American dream but few schools bother with teaching you how to build one.

Why is that? Everyone thinks owning a home matters.

Last year at Southern Illinois University I gave a workshop in what the basic skills of a good life are as I understand them. Toward the end a young man rose in back and shouted, "I'm twenty-five and I don't know how to do anything except pass tests! If the fan belt on my car broke on a lonely road in a snow storm I'd freeze to death. Why have you done this to me?"

He's right. I'm the one who did it as much as any other teacher who takes the time young people need to find out what really matters. I did it innocently, and desperately. Just trying to make a living.

The young man had two college degrees it turned out, and his degrees were shrieking at me that going to school really doesn't matter very much except in a fantasy sense — to do fantastic things nobody should bother to do. People who do very well in school, it's widely understood, have much more than their share of suicides, bad marriages, family problems, unstable friendships, feelings of meaninglessness, addictions, failures, heart bypasses, and general bad health. What on earth is going on? What did they miss by being well-schooled?

Does going to school matter if it uses up the time you need to learn to build a house? Or grow vegetables? Or make a dress? Or love your family hard enough you don't need to switch them on and off like a TV set? Education matters, of course, but only flim-flam artists try to convince you that school and education are the same thing.

So, what matters in a good life? The only things that matter in a bad life are power, revenge, and forgetting how awful you feel. When people living bad lives get control of government machinery we're all in deep trouble. That's the very best reason to keep the machinery of government just as weak as you possibly can, because people who lead bad lives turn up in charge of it with increasing frequency.

It surprises me how many graduates leave college just assuming they know what matters because they've watched a lot of TV or read a lot or got straight "A"s. The truth is, if we can believe advertisements, what matters to most Americans is personal ownership of machines: cooking machines, blending machines, sewing machines, driving machines, picture-taking machines, television machines, tooth-brushing machines, sound-recording machines, computing machines, machines to kill insects, deliver orgasms, illuminate, send voices through wires, slot machines, cutting machines, shooting machines, entertainment machines, and many more. And indirect control over more ambitious machines seems to matter a lot, too: flying machines, bombing machines, voting machines, heart and lung machines, and a great variety of other mechanical creations.

All these devices are meant to defeat what would otherwise occur naturally without them.

Something convinced us that what occurs naturally cannot be the way to a good life, hence these battalions of machines. What percentage of your life is spent talking to machines? Buying them, learning to use them, ministering to their needs, betraying them with even newer and newer machine loves. It takes a lot of time, but what does it take time away from? Machines are sold by promising more — more good things, more time for human interaction. Machines are sold by promising better — better meals, better stories, better personal appearance, better relationships. More and better, more and better.

Yet here we are, all of us, frantically lost in a tunnel of loneliness, cut off from each other, disliking ourselves, envying those with superior machines. Ugliness and sickness abounds in spite of medical machines and mechanical therapies. An astonishing amount of bad food is around in spite of food machines. And we have fewer and worse human ties than seems possible if machines justified the time and money spent on them. What is going on? How much do these essential machines matter? What are they essential for?

At mid-century we reached a point where we so little could bear intimate contact with living things in their messy reality as compared to the clean simplicity of machines that we became willing to lock old people away with strangers, to lock up our mothers and fathers, to create a good investment opportunity in warehousing for the old. We completed a complex circle in doing that, a circle begun a century earlier when we locked our young people away in warehouses with other strangers. Does it matter that our parents die among strangers and our children live penned up by strangers? Does that have an effect on the quality of life left theoretically "free" in the middle? What do you think? The assertion that isolation chambers for the young and old are an advance in human society doesn't square with any observed reality. It, too, is part of the great nonthought-of received ideas — like memorizing the significance of the space program. After you fall into the habit of accepting what other people tell you to think, you lose the power to think for yourself. I suspect that's why so few of us challenge the premises of old-age homes and schools.

Talking to machines makes us familiar with the way machines think; it makes us resist pondering the degree to which our own lives are mechanical and our own thought well-controlled like the thoughts of machines. Machines don't ever surprise you after you know their habits. Market research teaches that surprise can be bred out of human behavior, too.

Ken Kesey once wrote that Big Nurse had killed JFK and I want to argue that talking to machines when you should be talking to people and the natural world is what has clear-cut the Pacific forests, trashed the fish in Puget Sound, weakened the soil all over America, turned Cape Cod Bay into a dead sea, and burned gigantic holes in the stratosphere. Not a single one of those events matter at all to machinery, and since machinery is what we have been most intimate with since early childhood, they don't matter to us, either — regardless of what we say. At best we're ambivalent. Who in his right mind would live without an automobile? A computer? A telephone? A fax machine or a toaster? Relying on machines affects everyone who does it profoundly, seductive as it is to think it is you who are immune.

So far I've asked you to consider three aspects of modern American life we all think really matter: well-funded schools, the space program, and state-of-the-art technology. On close inspection all seem the obsessions of madmen more than parts of a good life or a good society. How did they come to matter when things that really matter don't?

In recent years we've heard that what really matters most is competing successfully in something called "the global economy." Try to pass over the fact that all economies are overwhelmingly national and the healthiest ones substantially local, and let's consider what you are being asked to believe. You are being asked to believe, in effect, that America's tremendous self-sufficiency in food doesn't matter; that the incredible abundance of fuels, fibers, metals, building materials, roads, technology, libraries, and labor we enjoy no longer matters; that in some mysterious way we are in danger of losing what matters because we are "noncompetitive." We already possess all the essentials for a good material life "in-house" as it were — what does this intimidating global economy exist for if not to produce and distribute material for a good fife? To what kind of human being does this economy really matter? It's easy to see how it would matter to machinery, with the urgencies of mechanism, but not clear what the point of it is for flesh and blood.

What if you forget "the planet" and concentrate on finding a place where you can feel at home for the rest of your life? What if you shape your work so that it serves your spirit, your loved ones, your friends and neighbors? Would it matter in the long run? What if you tend the land and water in your own neighborhood and feel good about it because it is the best and only service you can perform for Planet Earth?

Machines can be stored anywhere, can function anywhere, and are indifferent to the machines they associate with, but men and women must build the meanings of their lives around finding a few, a very few, people to touch and love and care for. If you fail in that it doesn't matter how well financed the school you went to was, how healthy the space program is, or how many machines you own — you'll be miserable. If this is so, and I confess it looks that way to me, you'll have to sabotage the global economy to survive as a human being, and you'll have to learn to think for yourself because schools and governments and machine-makers will lie to you about what matters every time.

Whatever you think about all this, the question "What matters?" can't be avoided. How can you steer a course for yourself until you answer it? Follow the path of experts in this and you're going to be in for a long series of unpleasant shocks because "What matters?" is plain and simple a religious question and machines don't know anything about answering such questions; nor do societies that pattern their workings after the logic of machinery as our own has done — at least since the turn of the century when the Supreme Court shocked the country by declaring that corporations were "persons" in the eyes of the law, enjoying all those human rights men and women did. You don't have to be a genius to see that when the ruler says a machine is a man, then it is only a little distance to discovering that a man is a machine.

At the transition to a new century you have to decide whether it matters or not to be a machine, and if you decide it does, you have to take the difficult step of establishing what it means to you to be a human being; in what way does that obligate you that being a machine doesn't? As so often happens, when you painfully decide you must think for yourself because the received thought of others is poisoning you, you will realize with a start that being human means exercising free will. And the only way that can happen is making your own commitments and paying the heavy price for honoring them. Otherwise you are a machine, predestined, no matter how light and free you feel for the moment.

If you think the meaning of life can be extracted from dramas of journalism like the space program, you end up strange and hollow, addicted to synthetic urgencies, causes, projects, labels, slogans, and synthetic thrills. If you think meaning can be determined by synthetic institutions like schools, political parties, hospitals, or central planners, you end up dumb, though perhaps a doctor of philosophy, sick, though well medicated, and indifferently housed, no matter how scientifically your domicile is put together.

Figure out what matters. Do it yourself; work hard at it; no one else can do it for you. Relying on others in this regard or ignoring the necessity will ruin you though you sit surrounded by machines in a rich school watching videos of spaceships. Each of us has a design problem to solve: to create from the raw material around us the curriculum for a good life. It isn't easy and it isn't the same for any two people. If you think you can buy it, look around you at the shambles my own generation has made of communal life and family life by trying to buy it or fashion it with machinery.

About 150 years ago we signed a Devil's Bargain — to destroy the earth, the forests, the air, and the water for money — a bargain in which our part entailed abandoning family life and neighborhood loyalties, locking up all the children and old people, keeping everyone useless out of the way while we made money. And some of us, at least, did make money, becoming rich and powerful enough to think of a global economy and a world order that would make us even richer. But it was a trick done with mirrors. We only pulled it off by spending the inheritance of the future. It's almost gone and there doesn't seem to be any easy way to get it back.

So here we are, rich and powerful — and it doesn't seem to matter any more than the gold of Midas did. Here we are unable to reach any of our national ideals, still as we were when we entered Western history: trying to find out what we are and what we will become.

Where do you start? First you have to find yourself. There isn't any other way. If you wait on that you'll be buried even deeper in the artificial programs of others. First you have to strip away decades of programming and overlays and discover your own outline beneath it all. It hurts to do that. This was once called "knowing yourself." Until you take that step there won't be any self to know, just a collection of relays and switches, sensors and twitches that can be manipulated by engineers you can't see. On the other hand, if you know what matters and are willing to fight and even die for it, nothing can colonize your mind and you will be truly a free spirit.

One important way men and women come to know themselves is to closely study their own families. People who run from that obligation will find no substitute for the missing knowledge. Another way lies in two types of critical decision which unmistakably define you: first, what you absolutely refuse to do, and second, what you eagerly choose to do. Acts of refusal. Acts of affirmation.

You affirm yourself best in solitudes and meditations, not in parties or frantic socializing. Solitude leads to depth of intellect, depth of heart, and often to piety. People who avoid solitude have a dependency disease that makes them dangerous.

The most radical act of refusal is to refuse to become a non-person as our expert-ridden technocratic society would have you be. Think of Mother Theresa. When she refused to admit that she was old and ugly and poor and powerless she forced the rest of us to acknowledge she wasn't any of those things.

Acts of affirmation and acts of refusal always matter. Refuse people who beg for help and you define the limit of your personal humanity, where flesh and blood gives way to the machine deep inside. Extending your hand in acts of affirmation enlarges the human zone and forces the machine inside you to break.

Learn to forgive and you enter an arena of spectacular affirmation. Begin by forgiving yourself, then forgive your family. You will have established a foundation for self-respect and categorical love by doing that — the kind that isn't given or removed by the logic of performance, but given freely, without conditions. If you affirm forgiveness you have the secret of eternal renewal so clearly described in the Christian Gospels. When you love people who hurt you, the effect is transcendental. You swell up with the power of being fully human and truly free. My own family taught me this in many ways; now forgiveness is one of the affirmations I struggle to practice. When I succeed I feel blessed. You might, too. It's worth a try.

To be real you need to celebrate your own history, humble and tormented as it might be, and the history of your own parents and grandparents, howsoever that history be marked by scars and mistakes. It is the only history you will ever have; reject it and you reject yourself. All the rest is the sickness of fantasy. Cherish what is yours; protect it; defend it; never accept the false evaluations of outsiders in regard to it. Whether your family is the best or the worst doesn't matter very much. Being first or last at anything truly doesn't matter, and your case will be hopeless as long as you think it does.

Refuse to be trivialized by an economic order that assigns important work to titles like "Doctor of Philosophy" instead of to men and women. Hold the authorities who clear-cut our forests and poison our water in contempt not awe.

Sabotage their undertakings in any way you can, even ways as small as misfiling their papers or dragging your feet on the way to jail. Keeping score by income and status is a mark of a limited mind; past a modest point your possessions, your machines, and your titles begin to own you. Past a modest point they dictate your behavior, consume your time, dominate your human relations — and when that happens you have become a machine, however well fed and secure you are. Instead, affirm a world of moral seriousness where everyday things are sacred to you. When that happens the leaves and grass and water sparkle and shine, lighting up the darkness. When that happens you are wealthy beyond measure.

Trust in yourself. Reject the insane claims that technological progress is human progress, that human destiny and machine improvement are wrapped up together in some way. They are not. The spirit of machinery seeks to infect living things and make them like machinery, too — that is, at the bottom of the cynical global system of industrial development. Better to be John Henry than the steam hammer; better to be an outlaw than a votary if it comes down to that. Live free or you won't really be alive at all. That, I can guarantee, really matters.

Reject people and institutions which teach you that nothing is sacred; their legacy has ruined minds and hearts and degraded our national culture. They have nothing to say that is true.

You'll have to decide quickly whether wealth really matters, but be careful before you answer. You live in history's wealthiest state locked in a consumption trance for over a hundred years — devouring its children, its families, its hills, sky, and water in order to buy machinery to talk to.

I hope you graduate to a different reality than this.

The Art of True Conversation: A Letter to My Daughter

Dear Kid,

I was talking with an old friend last night about some difficulties his son was having adjusting to being grown-up, when I realized with a start we were traveling in styles of conversation so disparate that our talk wouldn't help solve the young man's problem. My friend was self-expressing and doing it quite well. With care and precision he was rendering critical analyses and judgments at high speed, marked with intelligence, but like all judgmental discourse, clotted with unexamined values and assumptions. To complicate matters I was hooked, as usual, in a mode of talking designed to explore the mystery of where the kid had misstepped; why, and what payoff his present self-destructive course was delivering — for I believe strongly all behavior has its goal and if the goal of "bad" behavior can be determined, better substitutes might be possible.

But the final, unsolvable dilemma was that my friend misinterpreted my part of the dialogue as competition. Because of his necessary habit as a businessman, he unconsciously assumed he and I were in some sort of contest to determine who had the soundest strategy. An undertone of right/wrong made free testing of ideas, "probes," in McLuhan's useful metaphor, impossible. Rather than pushing out ideas for inspection, deferring judgment, asking questions to clarify, we were forced into caution by the powerful compulsion of keeping score on each other. This had to be a pure waste if the son's trouble was indeed what we were really talking about.

The frustrating situation I've just described happens all the time, of course. It probably happened to you recently whoever you are.

Rhetoric: A Lost Art

Beginning with Aristotle and the Greeks the Western world saw the study of how to speak and listen effectively as the quintessential human art. They called this pursuit "rhetoric," and though the meaning has degenerated in contemporary dictionaries into "the art of persuasion," that's an accountant's way to regard this central and peculiarly human undertaking. Korzybski and the general semanticists in this century, came to see the constellations of rhetoric as a *sine qua non* of sanity itself. Without accurate maps of each other we are condemned to wander in an infuriating wilderness.

Petrarch, Erasmus, Machiavelli, and other great names in the pantheon we call Renaissance humanists found an intimate link between rhetoric and moral growth. If you can't figure out the instrumentality of how the other guy is talking, you can't benefit fully from his experience or help him much with your own. However socially poised you appear to be, you are condemned to be one of the *isolani*, known only to yourself, knowing only yourself.

My friend and I had a missed connection in rhetoric last night — we couldn't adjust our wave lengths. For all the good we did his son we'd have been better discussing Phil Rizzuto and the Hall of Fame.

Social Talk

At baseball games and parties, in offices, bars, and on the street most of the talk we exchange with each other is social. Its varieties need to be matched up fairly closely among the talking partners or there is certain to be misunderstanding, hard feelings, and frustration. If one speaker is problem-solving, another is self-expressing (under the general guise of problem-solving), a third displaying his wit and joy at being alive, and a fourth playing for keeps by competing with the other three, trying to force a scorecard on the players, then you have emotional chaos, a type of chaos increasingly common among Americans who find themselves strangers to each other.

The appearance of sociability in such a situation masks a real condition of social starvation, one in which everybody goes home feeling lonely, angry, unfulfilled, too often to try again the next day in the same way, until finally company itself seems hardly worth the bother.

If you're able to recognize the main kinds of social talk, and you understand the utilities of each sort, you're in a better position to steer away from the shoals in a social ensemble and to exit the situation quickly when other people don't know how to participate. The first thing you need to understand are the various values to be gained from social talk. There are just two: to endow yourself with significance or to endow others. You do the latter by listening intelligently, asking intelligent questions, making intelligent and compassionate suggestions.

Five Flavors of Social Talk

1) Probably the commonest variety of this type of conversation is *self-expression*. Whether rendered as opinion, criticism, commentary, pontification, or whatever, it is really a way grownups say, "Me, me, me, me, me, and me!" In graceful doses it's useful to give your friends a fix on who you are, what you find important, what your code of values is proclaimed to be. Your behavior, of course, is the reality of your value code. The disparity between what you say you believe and what your actions say you believe is intensely interesting to people who must associate with you; in fact they should assume it measures your personal honesty.

2) Almost equally common is the practice of *recreating information* (often distorting it into disinformation): the weather, prices, bits of gossip, rules, headlines, reproducing editorial opinion that originated elsewhere, etc. Because so much information is in some measure false, even a short term evaluation of what you purvey establishes your reliability. Doesn't work to protest, "But they lied to me!" because your selection of sources of information to credit is a crucial measure of who you really are.

3) Probably next in order of frequency is *competition* as the purpose of conversation. You need only sit in an executive lunchroom or watering hole a few hours and eavesdrop to realize that whatever the seeming purpose of the group's conversation, the actual purpose is to establish who can dominate, who's second, who's last. "Winning" arguments, or preempting disproportionate time establishes aggressiveness and ambition in most cases; seldom is the triumphant party's case to be relied upon as "truth."

4) The grand bestower of significance on others is *expressions*

of curiosity. Whether verbal or nonverbal, it's the main way we confer the vital gift of importance on the people we talk to. If people don't ask questions about your life (outside the perfunctory) many things are measured: compassion, good will, concern, caring, and self (as in selfishness vs. selflessness).

5) Finally, I think, the last important component of social conversation is *entertainment*, by which I mean largely the power to see the world with humor and wit. The most cursory examination will show humor to be a refreshing questioning of literal, everyday reality. All kinds of humor, it makes no difference which, tell you social life is an illusion, a game, and however seriously one pursues the objectives of the game in times of trouble, tension, etc., it is always possible to step back and see the game, to place things in proportions that are proper. People whose humor is available to others consistently will never describe some action or threatened action as "ruining their life." They know better. The ability to entertain in social conversation (when not a form of self-expression) is a statement of one's ability to know reality. Humorless people are often recklessly bad judges of reality.

Spirit Talk

If you can practice the five forms of social conversation skillfully, you are indeed blessed. You'll certainly be sought after by all. And if that's all your conversation is, you'll also slowly petrify. After tens of thousands of practice sessions with each form their limited structures will be maddeningly familiar to you. You'll be led by your own mouth round and round in circles, on paths you've traveled many times before. No lasting satisfaction will derive from any social encounter, no evolution, no growth. The future will be exactly as present and past have been. Out of social conversation, if that's all there is, comes the barrenness and sterility of middle age.

Especially in the Anglo-Saxon world, where rhetoric was discarded by the philosophy of the Reformation, many of the young look at this interminable future of elaborate social conversation networks that industrial societies find vital to "business culture" with disgust. There is some fundamental and radical difference between the important talk of youth that makes love, friendship, and significance reasonably easy to reach, and the social conversation of older people, in particular of self-important older people, that makes it apparent these life-and-death qualities are very difficult to obtain in later life.

I hope you'll reread that last idea. It will help you understand why attractive young people in the United States, almost exclusively the sons and daughters of the prosperous, kill themselves in record numbers these days. Teenage suicide, occurring as it does in the classes who have "made it," is mute and powerful testimony to how sterile and inhuman a destination "making it" really can be. When children prefer death to the life of the future as they see it being lived by their fathers, mothers, and family friends, it's time to find the problem not in them but in us. I think the most important difference between the good lives of children and the lives of post-childhood people in the United States is the three flavors of conversation I want to call "spirit talk."

Anatomy of Spirit Talk

Just three streams of conversation are infinitely renewable, always fresh, always appropriate, always valuable — the possession of even one of these in your conversational repertory will keep you alive. To own all three is to be truly rich, self-sufficient, able to appreciate what a great gift life is.

1) The first of these kinds of spirit talk is the most easily obtainable and instantly rewarding. It arises from a real human need to be *emotionally generous*. It's fairly easy to spot people who aren't emotionally generous (though often such people are materially generous) because they gravitate to positions of power.

They may have a constitutional need to interfere in the lives of others, perhaps even claiming the interventions are in your best interests — even if you don't realize it now. Not all power positions are military, political, or industrial; social workers and schoolteachers, for example, customarily are small canvas power brokers. You can be in such a position and still be emotionally generous — constantly encouraging all those around you to reach for their best, and supporting them when they fall short without recrimination or lecture. It's not impossible, just unlikely in my experience. Those who manage both power and emotional generosity are a most valuable form of genius, and a fairly scarce breed as well.

Emotional generosity shows best and most reliably when the going is tough. Sweet, helpful, socially gregarious "nice" people who are quick with a kind word when you don't need it but scarce when your back is to the wall are obviously not the kind of emotionally generous conversationalists I mean.

The idea of emotional generosity to a degree that strengthens, ennobles, and exhilarates you on the giving end was caught well by the French thinker Simone Weil. She found even the thought of individuals so emotionally generous as to be able to help the afflicted ". . . a more astounding miracle than walking on water, healing the sick, or even raising the dead." Conversations in which you support others who behave horribly, without concern that your efforts are scorned or betrayed, or in which this miraculous kind of affection is not returned to you, are the therapeutic portion of spirit-conversation. If you have little of this in your makeup it might be something worth exploring.

2) Conversations where two or more people join in intense, high-focus interchanges in order to *solve a problem,* whether that problem is how to increase the sales of a business, air pollution, or to decide on what ethical grounds Phil Rizzuto could be admitted to the Hall of Fame, are incredibly interesting and satisfying whether you succeed in solving the problem or not. All lasting human connections — marriages, friendships, partnerships, living communities — are only possible to those who constantly solve and re-solve the problem of entropy, the drift toward boredom, the mistaken belief there is nothing left to discover in each other.

When nature is left to take her course, relationships always dissolve and disintegrate. How many times does that have to happen before you become unable to invest much intensity in any sort of human connection because you expect, from experience, that even the most exciting beginnings must end in ennui? The answer is — not many. If you learn to make the search for solutions a part of every human encounter, you'll find the lightweight crowd beginning to avoid you, it's true; on the other hand those engagements that survive, and the new ones which pass through your screens, folks capable of spirit-conversation, have a wonderfully nourishing kind of conversation to exchange with you. Both parties to your dialogue will remember what was said for a long time. They'll think about it, dwell on it, worry it as a lively dog does a bone. They'll look forward to seeing you again, and you them.

Notice the search-for-solutions mode of talk is inexhaustible. Unlike the five forms of social conversation, it's hard to put a limit on the power of this sort of excavating to turn up pay dirt. People who are in the habit this way generally find they physically wear out and break off the dialogue long before the practice of talking in this fashion loses its savor. If you're searching for solutions with an emotionally generous partner, it's pretty near impossible not to begin to feel excitement in the undertaking.

3) The third flavor of spirit talk is far and away the most essential to understand, to grow and change constantly, to evolve into the kind of calm, wise, courageous soul you could scarcely even imagine in earlier days. I'll call this mode of conversation *exploration of the mystery*, or *search for meaning*, as a label would perhaps shed additional light on the processes taking place.

If you aren't completely mechanized by the drab routines of your life (and I am especially directing this to "successful" people who appear to lead colorful, interesting lives, but in their innermost heart are well aware they function mostly as an apparatus, learning nothing and teaching nothing, only accumulating and outwitting others) you'll be able to recall a time in your youth when everything seemed fresh, significant, interesting, awesome — when life was seemingly larger than life.

You will have been told at different times those feelings are

the special province of children and must be put away in adulthood for practical reasons. You will also, no doubt, have occasionally encountered someone who hasn't put aside the fundamental
understanding that life is a great mystery, that the planet whirling
through space is a big mystery, that the immense weight of the polar
icecaps is a mystery, that the unbelievable homing ability of the
giant sea turtle is yet another, *ad infinitum.*

What should your few years of life be "about?" What is the
value and meaning of family? Of loyalty? Of sexual encounters?
Why do you seek to "make love?" No job, no patriotism, no religion, no disease, no one you'll ever know and nothing you ever
can be is as interesting, as significant, and as capable of yielding
enormous, lasting pleasure to you as the relentless, unending pursuit of mysteries.

"Practical" people, by which one usually marks the most mechanical of machine-people, are content to delegate the exploration of mysteries to their parson, priest, or rabbi. One of those, in
turn, will possess several purchased anthologies of approved
mystery-sermons which will be rendered in mellifluous prose at
appropriate moments. In fact, such behaviors are a dissipation of
the mystery-search you need to maintain to be fully human. The
questions and observations, the detection of mysterious patterns,
linkages, odd emblems, unexplained coincidences, must be an ever-
ready, ever-present part of your intake and processing system, and
of your rhetoric.

If you can build a society of emotionally generous, search-
for-solution friends who understand and venerate the mystery

search as the single most important aspect of intelligent, satisfying life you've found the greatest engine possible to sustain the wonder of childhood for a lifetime. Indeed, if you can find two souls whose conversation is sprinkled with insights about mystery, and whose curiosity about your own insights is lively and eager, you own a treasure whose worth is beyond valuation.

Are there really any answers to big questions? Of course there are. They are private answers, as individualized as your own fingerprint is from everybody else's. The answers come slowly, and only after very, very hard work, not by a priest but by yourself. When you own even a part of an answer, the quiet strength you gain in every attitude of daily living is a great comfort in times of trial.

Am I maintaining the best, most satisfying conversations are "religious" conversations? Not exactly. To begin with, in my own experience, regular church, temple, synagogue, and mosque goers are the least attuned to mysteries of anybody. Often they've turned the key over to a hired gun, a paid stranger. It doesn't work very well in my experience, although a congregation is a wonderful thing in itself. However saintly the experience of hearing someone else tell you about mystery makes you feel, the good feeling wears off quickly; you have to look for yourself if you want it to last.

Constant awareness of just how very strange *everything* is sharpens your conversational sensibilities wonderfully, sends you poking into nooks and crannies of subjects for clues overlooked, and makes you wary of prefabricated arguments.

A few friends willing to stargaze with you from time to time forges a subversive society very difficult to condition or to intimidate, because the practice of keeping alive the awareness that mystery is central to human existence makes both the rewards and the punishments of others hold very little meaning. Or, at the very least, become secretly funny.

I hope you'll think about these things long enough to figure out who you and your friends usually are in conversation, and whether that's really who you need to be.

Much love,

The Educated Person

Here I've used the old-fashioned "he," but mean both sexes.

1. An educated person writes his own script through life. He is not a character in anyone else's play, nor does he mouth the words of any intellectual's utopian fantasy. He is self-determined.

2. Time does not hang heavily on an educated person's hands. He can be alone. He is never at a loss for what to do with time.

3. An educated person knows his rights and knows how to defend them.

4. An educated person knows the ways of the human heart; he is hard to cheat or fool.

5. An educated person possesses useful knowledge: how to build a house, a boat, how to grow food, etc.

6. An educated person possesses a blueprint of personal value, a philosophy. This philosophy tends toward the absolute; it is not plastic or relative, altering to suit circumstances. Because of this an educated person knows at all times who he is, what he will tolerate, where to find peace. But at the same time an educated person is aware of and respects community values and strange values.

7. An educated person can form healthy attachments wherever he is because he understands the dynamics of relationships.

8. An educated person accepts and understands his own mortality and its seasons. He understands that without death and ag-

ing nothing would have any meaning. An educated person learns from all his ages, even from the last minutes of his life.

9. An educated person can discover the truth for himself. He has intense awareness of the profound significance of *being*, and the profound significance of being *here*.

10. An educated person can figure out how to be useful to others, and in trading time, insight, and service to meet the needs of others, he can earn the material things he needs to sustain a wholesome life.

11. An educated person has the capacity to create new things, new experiences, new ideas.

Sources

Many of the essays and speeches in this collection have previously appeared in print. Some have been published in established educational journals and magazines, and their places of appearance are listed below. All the pieces have been edited somewhat for this volume.

Part One

"The Curriculum of the Family" originally appeared in *Teacher* magazine in August 1990,

"A Year with John Taylor Gatto" by Jamaal M. Watson, was published in *Children's Express Quarterly,* Spring 1991.

Part Two

"Universal Education" was published in *YES! A Journal of Positive Futures,* Winter 1998/1999 .

"How Public Are Our Public Schools?" was published in *The Threefold Review,* Summer 1992.

"Nine Assumptions and Twenty-One Facts" was published in *SKOLE: The Journal of Alternative Education, Summer, 1995.*

"A Different Kind of Teacher" was published under the title "Bitter Lessons: What's Wrong with American Teachers," in *The Sun,* December 1993.

Part Three

"In Defense of Original Sin" was published in *The Sun,* January 1998.

"The Art of True Conversation" was published in *The Journal of Family Life*, Volume 3, Number 2, 1997.

About the Author

John Taylor Gatto was a teacher in the New York City public school system for thirty years. A graduate of Columbia University, he was named, by various organizations, New York City Teacher of the Year in 1989, 1990, and 1991, and New York State Teacher of the Year in 1990 and 1991. Shortly after receiving this last award, he publicly resigned from teaching through an op-ed piece published in *The Wall Street Journal*, and began to speak and write on schooling issues. By the year 2000 he had traveled over a million miles in fifty states and seven foreign countries, bearing witness to what he had seen as a schoolteacher, and what we might do about it. The power of his ideas has placed him at the center of the national education reform debate.

Gatto is the author of the bestselling *Dumbing Us Down: The Hidden Curriculum of Compulsory Schooling, The Exhausted School*, and *The Underground History of American Education*. He serves on the Advisory Boards of the National TV-Turnoff and the National Council of Alternative Community Schools. In 1998 he received the Alexis de Toqueville Award for his contribution to the cause of human liberty. His articles have appeared in *The Wall Street Journal, The New York Times, Whole Earth Review, The Sun, The Utne Reader*, and many other periodicals. He can be contacted through the Odysseus Group, 295 East 8th Street, New York, New York 10009.